# First Published in 2019 by America's Food Hub

## © 2019 Suzy Shaw

### All rights reserved.

America's Food Hub
Titangate Press
12 Steinway Ave
New York, NY, 10034

*America's Food Hub is an imprint of Titangate Press*

**British Library Cataloging in Publication Data**
A catalogue record for this book is available from the British Library.
Repository XI, Domicile 23, Data Bank 2—Cooking Manuals

**Library of Congress Cataloging in Publication Data**
Suzy Shaw, 2019—Index 22a, Cookbooks & Household Media

ISBN: 9781076089540

**Front, interior, & back design**
By Excelsior Fonts, 1 Rockwell Ave, New York, NY, 10504

**Printed in the United States of America**
By Amazon and its affiliates, 410 Terry Ave, North, Seattle, WA, 98109-5210

**TITANGATE
PRESS**

# PREFACE

**M**aster your Air Fryer with affordable, quick & easy meals! In this #1 best seller, you'll learn how to cook 2019's most affordable, quick & easy 5-ingredient Air Fryer recipes on a budget. Do you want to cook with your Air Fryer but don't know where to start? Quit worrying! In this cookbook, you'll learn how to not only start, but love, your Air Fryer, which will guide you to amazing meals in the most affordable, quick & easy way possible. Along the way, you'll learn to cook only the highest quality 5-ingredient Air Fryer recipes, offering tons of scientifically proven health benefits, such as improving your appetite, cholesterol, blood pressure and reversing diabetes. Rest assured, you, the Air Fryer beginner, will get the healthy body you have always dreamt of! Each recipe includes...

- ✓ **5-ingredients or less:** cut expensive and hard to find ingredients from your diet.
- ✓ **Affordable ingredients:** save money cooking budget friendly recipes.
- ✓ **Nutritional information:** keep track of your daily calories.
- ✓ **Servings:** cook the right amount of food for your diet.
- ✓ **Cooking times:** save time in the kitchen.
- ✓ **Highly rated recipes:** enjoy only the highest quality recipes.

Pick up your copy today and start cooking amazing Air Fryer recipes that cater for the diverse needs of you and your family, allowing you, the Air Fryer beginner, to save time, money and stress in the kitchen.

Warm Regards,

*Suzy Shaw*

Nutritionist & Diet Coach, MD.
America's Food Hub.

# CONTENTS

## AIR FRYER GUIDE

## AIR FRYER FATS

## AIR FRYER SUCCESS

## BREAKFASTS & BRUNCH

## BEEF, PORK & LAMB

## SEAFOOD

## VEGAN & VEGETARIAN

## SNACKS & SIDE DISHES

# DESSERTS

# AIR FRYER INTRODUCTION

Simply put, air-fried foods are healthier because they don't use all that oil! They cook with nature's simplicity—hot air!

-SUZY SHAW

# AIR FRYER

## IT'S ALL HOT AIR

The big day has arrived! You finally have your hands on your shiny new Air Fryer. But you're probably wondering what it is and how to get set up. No worries, this chapter is designed with beginners in mind. First, let's begin by talking about the Air Fryer in general. Simply put, an Air Fryer is a countertop convection oven that cooks food with hot air. This is great because it means you can cook food affordably, quickly and easily! I personally think the term "air fryer" is misleading because people get confused by the old-fashioned air fryer that your grandma might have in her pantry. The big difference, however, between these two types of fryer is that the modern air fryer does not require huge amounts of oil because it cooks food with only hot air—nothing else is required! So, hopefully you have learned that the Air Fryer cooks food by circulating hot air around using a convection mechanism. Enough of the interesting science, for now.

Did you forget to prepare something for dinner? No problem—the Air Fryer can cook such lovely delicious food in just moments! Such scrumptious food includes sizzling burgers and dry crispy fries– super affordable, quick & easy too! What's more? When your fryer finishes cooking, the latent heat inside keeps your food warm. I can confidently say that my air fryer has changed the way I cook because I now spend less time in the kitchen and more time doing the things I enjoy, like spending precious time with family and walking my dogs. In fact, even my weekly shop at my local grocery store is super cheap and easy. I fill my grocery basket to the brim with all kinds of locally sourced, affordable and easy to find ingredients which I whack into my Air Fryer, allowing me to whip up amazing meals for my family to enjoy.

Every week, I love frying a batch of burgers for a quick 'on-the-go' lunch after I take my grandchildren to school. What's great is the temperature control on my Air Fryer dial because it means I can have it all cooked for when I return home. In fact, I whack all manner of things in the frying basket on a low temperature because my Fryer keeps it warm for hours. This appliance has revolutionized how I cook, and I have even retired my once beloved Instant Pot back to the pantry.

# AIR FRYER SAFETY

You, like most people, are probably wondering why I would want an Air Fryer? I mean, aren't they those machines that explode oil on the countertop? Well, that might have been the case for old-fashioned fryers, but this is not one of those! Rest assured, a modern Air Fryer comes equipped with loads of safety features. For example, it is physically impossible to to open the frying basket without pressing the lock button first, either naturally or manually—so burning hazards are minimized! This is great to know if you have small children around the house. Indeed, modern day Air Fryers are quiet, safe and easy to use. In fact, the US government recognizes their safety and so they even have 10 UL Certified proven safety mechanisms to prevent most issues. So, Air Fryers are a very safe appliance to have around your kitchen provided, of course, you use your common sense. Importantly, mop up any water spillages close to your fryer and keep it away from children, pets and vulnerable people at all times. For your safety, I have compiled a list of steps below that you should follow when using your Air Fryer.

1  Your Air Fryer gets hot. Do not touch any of its surfaces when its cooking. When cooking is done, use oven mitts or potholders to touch it and wait for it to cool down.

2  Avoid immersing the cord, plug or the Air Fryer unit in water or other liquid due to electric shocks.

3  Persons with reduced physical, sensory or mental capabilities, or lack of experience and knowledge, should not use your Air Fryer without supervision.

4  Always keep children away from your Air Fryer.

5  Avoid using your Air Fryer if it has a damaged plug or power cord.

6  Avoid using your Air Fryer outdoors due to adverse weather conditions.

7  Avoid letting the cord hang over the edge of the table or countertop, especially if you have pets around the house.

8  Avoid placing your Air Fryer near hot gas or electric burner.

9  Ensure that both the timer dial and temperature dial are OFF when disconnecting your Air Fryer from the power outlet.

10  Ensure that the frying basket is locked into position when turning on your Air Fryer.

11  Ensure that the frying basket drawer is fully closed, and the handle locked securely in the drawer when using your Air Fryer.

12  Carefully handle your Air Fryer after frying because the frying basket and the food inside of it are extremely hot.

# CONTROL DIALS

Now that you've got to know more about your Air Fryer, I have included a picture below that shows you what a typical Air Fryer looks like and all its different parts. The Air Fryer in this picture is a standard model you might find online or in your department store. It is by no means typical of what your Air Fryer might look like. Rather, it is intended to give you a general idea of the different parts to your Air Fryer.

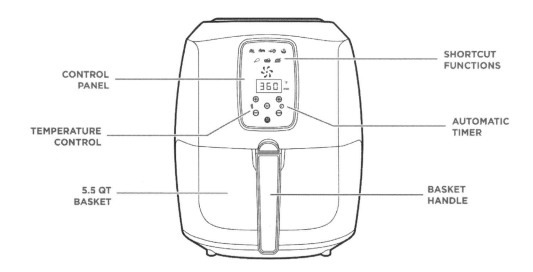

1  The Temperature Control Dial allows you to select frying temperatures from 175°F to 400°F. Temperatures can be adjusted at any time during the cooking period.

2  The Control Panel shows the HEAT ON light when cooking temperature is reached. It also shows the Red POWER light, which will turn on when you ise your Fryer. The shortcut functions are specifically designed for certain kinds of food, like poultry and fish, and you can select these if you think they are a better option than manually setting the frying temperature.

3  The Automatic Timer button allows you to select how long your food will cook for and will automatically count down during the cooking period. Typically, one beep sounds when frying time has reached 0 minutes.

# AIR FRYER PREP

So, now that you know a little more about your Air Fryer, it is time to get it prepped and ready for frying. I have complied a list of steps below which you should follow to avoid damaging your Air Fryer or causing yourself injury.

1 So, your Air Fryer is all boxed up in front of you. The first thing you should do is to assess the situation. What does your box look like? How big is it?

2 Your Air Fryer will come with warning cards and warning labels. Read these carefully.

3 Now carefully take your Air Fryer out of its box and remove all the warning stickers/cards on it.

4 Approach the front of your Air Fryer and firmly grip the frying basket handle to open the frying basket drawer. Remove the frying basket from your Air Fryer and place it on a flat, clean countertop.

5 Ensure that there is no packaging of any kind under and around the frying basket drawer.

6 Wash the frying basket and drawer in hot, soapy water. Dry all parts thoroughly with a kitchen towel.

7 WARNING: DO NOT immerse the main Air Fryer unit in water.

8 Lock frying basket into the drawer—you should hear a seal/click when it is locked securely in place.

# YOUR FIRST MEAL

Are you feeling hungry? Well, I am! Now that you have prepped your Air Fryer, it is time to start cooking amazing recipes. The steps below will guide you to cook your first meal.

1 Place your Air Fryer on a kitchen countertop next to a power outlet.

2 Grip the frying basket handle and remove the frying basket. Carefully place it on a flat countertop.

3 Choose your recipe and toss in your food/ingredients into the frying basket. For proper cooking, do not overfill the basket.

4 Put the frying basket back into your Air Fryer, making sure you hear a nice audible click/lock sound.

5 Plug your Air Fryer into the nearest power outlet.

6 Following your recipe instructions, choose an air frying temperature between 175°F to 400°F.

7   Following your recipe instructions, choose a cooking time using the temperature control dial. Your Air Fryer may illuminate when this cooking temperature is reached. **Optional:** Halfway through cooking, you might want to open the frying basket and give it a good shake to ensure even, consistent cooking.

8   When cooking is done, you Air Fryer may make a beeping noise. Wait for it to cool down.

9   Using oven mitts, open the drawer and shake the frying basket vigorously to see if your food is cooked properly.

10  If satisfied, remove the frying basket from your Air Fryer and place it on a flat countertop.

11  Using kitchen utensils, scoop/take out the food from the frying basket and place it onto a plate.

12  Unplug your Air Fryer when finished. You can also cover it using a range of jazzy Air Fryer covers available online at Amazon.

# HELPFUL HINTS

Are you full up after that amazing first meal? I certainly am. I have put together some steps below which you can follow when cooking your other meals.

1   I have found over the years that a dash of olive oil or vegetable oil works well for air frying because it gives the food a tasty golden brown appearance. Of course, using oil is entirely optional as your Air Fryer is designed to cook without it. You should follow your recipe instructions for more information on this.

2   Never overfill the frying basket with food because doing so results in poorly and unevenly cooked food. As a rule, I never go over the 2/3 mark when I'm filling the basket.

3   For the best cooking results, certain types of foods (i.e. vegetables) need to be shaken vigorously or turned over halfway through cooking. See your recipe for more information on this.

4   Sometimes smoke might happen and set off your fire alarm when you're cooking high fat foods like chicken wings, sausages and other meats. To avoid this, you can empty your frying basket of oil halfway through the cooking period (it is the excess oil that causes the smoke!)

5   Spray your food with oil and pat it dry before cooking to ensure browning—works well with fish and chicken recipes.

6   Your Air Fryer can reheat previously cooked/refrigerated food. Set the temperature to 300ºF for up to 10 minutes. Ensure the food is piping hot all the way through to avoid food poisoning.

# AIR FRYER CLEANING

So, you've been cooking with your Air Fryer for some time now and have noticed that it needs a good cleaning. I have put together 10 steps you should follow to clean your Air Fryer.

1   The frying basket may be coasted in grease from repeated and frequent use. Smoking can occur when bits of burnt food get recooked many times. So, you should get into the habit of cleaning your frying basket after every use.

2   The pan, basket and the inside of the appliance have a non-stick coating, so you should avoid using abrasive materials to clean them.

3   Wipe the outside of the appliance with a damp kitchen towel.

4   Clean the frying basket with hot water, some washing-up liquid and a nonabrasive sponge. You can use a degreasing agent to remove grease and grime. Hint: The frying basket is dishwasher-proof.

5   Clean the inside of your Air Fryer (after you have taken out the frying basket) with warm water and a non-abrasive sponge.

6   Clean the heating element with a cleaning brush to remove any food residues.

7   Push the cord into the cord storage compartment. Fix the cord by inserting it into the cord fixing slot.

8   When not in use, cover your Fryer with a jazzy cover to avoid dust accumulation.

# AIR FRYER FATS

Fats are integral to Air Frying. In addition to consuming high proportions of fats, it is vital that you make sure you are consuming the right varieties. Let's cut through all the confusion surrounding the good and bad kinds of fat and discuss which fats you should be aiming to integrate into your frying. We divide the 'good fats' into four distinct categories:

1  **SATURATED FATS**
2  **MONOUNSATURATED FATTY ACIDS (MUFAS)**
3  **POLYUNSATURATED FATTY ACIDS (PUFAS)**
4  **TRANS FATS (NATURALLY OCCURRING)**

All fats constitute a combination of the above varieties but are named according to the kind that is most dominant in their makeup. We will now take a look at each type of fat and consider which ones you should be including as part of your frying recipes. This way, you will be able to make quick and informed decisions as to how best to fuel your mind and body.

## SATURATED FATS

Saturated fats get a bad rep – many of us have been advised to avoid them because of the potential harmful effects they can have on our heart health. However, recent research has shown that there is no strong correlation between saturated fats and heart disease. After all, saturated fats have been a major component of the human diet for millennia. There are in fact numerous ways in which saturated fats can be advantageous to us.

Some foods with saturated fats in them contain medium-chain triglycerides (MCTs), particularly coconut oil, butter and palm oil. MCTs are easily digestible and are converted to energy in the liver. As a result, they are highly beneficial to those who want to lose weight or improve their performance during physical activity.

Here are some further benefits:

✓ Boosted immune system.
✓ Improved HDL-to-LDL cholesterol ratio.
✓ Improved bone density.
✓ Increased levels of HDL cholesterol to remove LDL from the arteries.
✓ Increased production of important hormones like cortisol and testosterone.

Foods which are rich in saturated fats include:

✓ Butter

- ✓ Cocoa butter
- ✓ Coconut oil
- ✓ Cream
- ✓ Eggs
- ✓ Lard
- ✓ Palm oil
- ✓ Red meat

# MONOUNSATURATED FATS

Monounsaturated fatty acids (MUFAs) differ from saturated fats in that they are pretty much universally embraced as a 'good' kind of fat. Numerous studies have revealed a link between MUFAs and certain positive outcomes like insulin resistance and good cholesterol. Other health benefits include:

- ✓ Lower blood pressure
- ✓ Decreased risk of developing heart disease
- ✓ Decrease in belly fat

The best sources of MUFAs are:

- ✓ Avocados and avocado oil
- ✓ Extra virgin olive oil
- ✓ Lard and bacon fat
- ✓ Macadamia nut oil

# POLYUNSATURATED FATS

How you prepare foods containing polyunsaturated fatty acids (PUFAs) is critical. When PUFAs are subjected to heat, they can create free radicals (uncharged molecules) which cause inflammation and have even been linked to cancer and heart disease. This means that for the most part PUFAs should be eaten cold, and never cooked.

You can get PUFAs from processed oils and other heart-friendly sources. The right kinds of PUFAs have immense health benefits when adopted into a balanced diet. Some such fats are Omega 3 and Omega 6, which are the primary components of many superfoods such as salmon and flaxseed.

Integrating PUFAs into your diet is therefore crucial. An ideal ratio of Omega 3 to Omega 6 stands at around 1:1 – however, most Westerners consume a ratio of 1:30! A good balance between Omega 3 and Omega 6 greatly decreases the risk of developing the following:

- ✓ Autoimmune disorders and other inflammatory diseases
- ✓ Heart disease
- ✓ Stroke
- ✓ Depression and ADHD

PUFA-rich foods include:
- ✓ Avocado oil
- ✓ Chia seeds
- ✓ Extra virgin olive oil
- ✓ Flaxseeds and flaxseed oil
- ✓ Sesame oil
- ✓ Walnuts

# TRANS FATS

You might double-take at seeing trans fats listed as 'good' fats, but they do in fact have a right to be termed as such. Though most trans fats are indeed unhealthy, one particular naturally occurring variety is decidedly beneficial: vaccenic acid. Vaccenic acid can be absorbed from grass-fed meats and dairy products.

The potential health benefits of this type of trans fat include:
- ✓ Lower risk of developing diabetes and obesity
- ✓ Lower risk of developing heart disease
- ✓ Protection against cancer

The best sources of healthy and natural trans fats are:
- ✓ Butter
- ✓ Yogurt
- ✓ Grass-fed animal products

# BAD FATS

Many people are drawn to the frying because it permits you to eat foods that, being high in fat, are satisfying and delicious. However, the idea that frying cooks can consume all the fat they want is a common misconception. On the contrary, there are several 'bad fats' which you should take the utmost care to avoid if you wish to achieve the best possible results. Remember, the quality of the food you eat should always be a number-one priority.

**Processed Trans and Polyunsaturated Fats**: You may be familiar with these kinds of fats, as they are present in many of the sweet and snack foods many of us enjoy. You may also already know that they are extremely damaging to your physical well-being. Artificial trans fats are the product of the processing of polyunsaturated fats. For this reason, you must try to consume only unprocessed PUFAs that have not been heated or modified in any way.

Trans fats are particularly harmful as they may lead to:

- ✓ An increased risk of cancer
- ✓ An increased risk of heart disease
- ✓ Inflammatory health issues
- ✓ A decrease in HDL cholesterol and an increase of LDL cholesterol

Here are some common sources of trans fats which you should aim to cut from your diet:
- ✓ Hydrogenated and partially hydrogenated oils that are in processed products like cookies, crackers, margarine, and fast food.
- ✓ Processed vegetable oils like cottonseed, sunflower, safflower, soybean, and canola oil.

# CONCLUSION

Saturated fats are not the boogeymen they've often been portrayed to be, but the best fats are those which are unprocessed. Processed and packaged foods are major stoppers to weight loss and heart health, so avoid them at all costs. At the end of the day, the main objective of Air Frying is to improve your overall well-being. This involves not only maintaining a good macro ratio but selecting the right kinds of foods for your health and physical condition.

# AIR FRYER SUCCESS

The Air Fryer doesn't come without its stumbling blocks, so here are some essential tips for staying on track as you progress further down the frying road.

- ✓ **HYDRATION:** As always, we should stress the importance of keeping yourself hydrated. Specifically, you should aim to drink at least 32 ounces of water within the first hour after waking up in the morning, and another 32-48 ounces before midday. Before the day ends, you should strive to drink at least half your body weight in water – ideally, close to your entire body weight.

- ✓ **PRACTICE INTERMITTENT FASTING**: Before jumping straight in, steadily reduce your carb intake in the days leading up to your fast days. Fast days should be divided into two phases:

- ✓ **BUILDING PHASE:** The period of time between your first and last meal.

- ✓ **CLEANING PHASE:** The period of time between your last and first meal. To start, try a cleaning phase of between 12 and 16 hours and a building phase of between 8 and 12 hours. As your body adjusts to the change, you will find yourself in a position to tackle a 4-6-hour building time and an 18-20-hour cleaning phase.

- ✓ **CONSUME SALT:** Too much sodium is generally deemed as unhealthy. However, a low-carb diet necessitates a high salt intake, as this type of regimen reduces your insulin levels and flushes out higher amounts of sodium from your kidneys. As a result, your sodium/potassium ratio is disrupted. Here are some tips to counteract this change:

- ✓ **EXERCISE REGULARLY:** Daily rigorous exercise can help activate glucose molecules called GLUT-4 which are needed to return glucose to fat and muscle tissues. Additionally, it can double the amount of protein present in both the liver and the muscles.

- ✓ **WATCH HOW MUCH PROTEIN YOU EAT:** Protein is integral to Air Fryer cooking but maintaining a proper balance is a must. If you eat too many protein-rich foods, you will end up converting the amino acids into glucose (through a process called gluconeogenesis). In the initial stages of your frying, vary the amounts of protein you consume in order to get a feel of how much is too much.

✓ **PICK YOUR CARBS WISELY:** The few carb-rich foods you do consume should be selected very carefully. It is best to stick to starchy veggies and fruits like berries, apples, lemons, and oranges. For a quick morning hit, blend them into a healthy green smoothie.

✓ **TAKE MCT OIL:** High-quality MCTs are extremely effective in replenishing the energy levels you deplete through the day. MCT oil can be used for cooking, as well as added to beverages like coffee, tea, smoothies, protein shakes, and so on.

✓ **MINIMIZE YOUR STRESS:** Stress is a major factor in decreased energy levels, so constant stress may serve as a threat to your cooking success. If you find yourself especially prone to stress at the moment, it may be wise to avoid dieting until you're in a better position to deal with the blow to your energy levels.

✓ **IMPROVE THE QUALITY OF YOUR SLEEP:** Sleep is essential for managing stress, among other things. Make sure your bedroom is conducive to a good night's rest. This means sleeping in a comfortable bed, in a darkened room no warmer than 70 degrees. Most adults function best on 7 to 9 hours of sleep every night, though a particularly stressful lifestyle may require even longer.

✓ **EAT GHEE:** Ghee works well as a butter substitute, as it can be used in more or less all the same ways and is exponentially healthier. Try frying meat or vegetables in it for a high-fat, healthy meal.

✓ **SEEK OUT OMEGA 3S:** If you find it hard to integrate Omega-3-rich foods into your diet, then you might consider taking supplements. You should make sure your Omega 3 intake matches your Omega 6s. Omega 3 is an extremely beneficial kind of fat, which is crucial to healthy frying.

✓ **AVOID ALCOHOL:** It may be hard to kiss the booze goodbye, but it is well-attested that alcohol impedes weight loss. Stay focused on your goals and order a glass of tonic water at the bar instead.

✓ **DRINK LEMON WATER:** Lemon water is a tasty and refreshing alternative to tap water that has the added benefit of balancing your pH levels.

✓ **AVOID 'SUGAR-FREE' PRODUCTS:** These labels may sound appealing but the vast majority of products advertised as 'sugar-free' or 'light' contain more carbs than the original!

✓ **BUY A FOOD SCALE:** Food scales are a great utensil to keep handy in your kitchen as they help you to accurately monitor what you are putting into your body. They are indispensable in tracking your carb and overall caloric intake. Invest in your success – get a high-quality, durable scale with a conversion button, automatic shutdown, tare function, and a removable plate.

✓ **STAY CARB-SAVVY:** To tackle the inevitable carb cravings, it is a good idea to make yourself aware of the many alternatives that exist. When the urge to order a bucket of fried chicken or a box of pad Thai arises, fight back with these tasty and healthy substitutes:

✓ **SHIRATAKI NOODLES** are made from yams and make a great low-carb alternative to pasta.

✓ **CAULIFLOWER RICE,** basically shredded cauliflower, mimics the texture and neutral taste of white or brown rice.

✓ **SPAGHETTI SQUASH** can be cut into the shape of noodles with the aid of a spiralizer or a fork. It tastes great and amounts to less than half the carbs and calories of conventional noodles.

✓ **HEAVY WHIPPING CREAM** or **ALMOND MILK** go great in your coffee instead of regular creamer, which is rich in calories.

# BREAKFASTS & BRUNCH

"Your morning sets up the success of your day. So many people wake up and check text messages, emails, and social media. I use my first hour awake for my morning routine of breakfast and meditation to prepare myself."

- SUZY SHAW

# Bell Pepper Eggs

**THE 4 SERVINGS CONTAIN: 311 CAL, 16.6 G FAT, 22.9 G PROTEIN, 2.6 G NET CARBS.**

## Ingredients

- ✓ Mild shredded cheddar, 1 c
- ✓ 8 Eggs
- ✓ Chopped medium onion, .25
- ✓ Chopped cooked ham, 3 oz
- ✓ Bell peppers, 4

## Method

1. Slice the tops off of the bell peppers. Scoop out the innards using a small knife. Divide the onion and ham into each pepper.

2. Crack two eggs into each pepper and top each with a quarter cup of cheese. Carefully place the peppers into the frying basket of your air fryer.

3. Set your air fryer to 390 °F and cook for 15 minutes.

4. When cooked, the peppers should be tender, and the eggs set.

5. Serve and enjoy.

# Southwest Ham & Egg Cups

**THE 2 SERVINGS CONTAIN: 3181 CAL, 23.5 G FAT, 28.3 G PROTEIN, 3.1 G NET CARBS.**

## Ingredients

- ✓ Shredded sharp cheddar cheese, .5 c
- ✓ Diced white onion, 2 tbsp.
- ✓ Dice bell pepper, .33 c
- ✓ 4 Eggs
- ✓ Sliced deli ham, 4 1-oz slices

## Method

1. Place a slice of ham into the bottom of four heat-safe molds.

2. Beat the onion, peppers and eggs together in a bowl.

3. Divide the mixture between the molds. Top with a sprinkling of cheddar cheese. Carefully place the molds inside your air fryer.

4. Set your fryer's temperature to 320 °F and cook for 12 minutes or until the tops are golden and the eggs are completely set.

5. Serve hot.

# Spicy Egg Cups

**THE 2 SERVINGS CONTAIN: 353 CAL, 24.3 G FAT, 20 G PROTEIN, 1.8 G NET CARBS.**

## Ingredients

- ✓ 4 Eggs
- ✓ Shredded sharp cheddar cheese, .5 c
- ✓ Full-fat cream cheese, 2 oz.
- ✓ Chopped pickled jalapenos, .25 c

## Method

1. Mix the eggs together in a bowl and divide between four silicone cupcake tins.

2. Using a microwaveable bowl, toss in the cheddar cheese, cream cheese, and jalapenos. Microwave this mixture for 30 seconds and then stir together. Divide the mixture between the four silicone molds. Try to get the mixture into the center of the eggs.

3. Place the molds in the basket of your air fryer.

4. Set your fryer's temperature to 320 °F and cook for ten minutes.

5. Serve while hot.

# Breakfast Soufflé

**THE 4 SERVINGS CONTAIN: 194 CAL, 14 G FAT, 8 G PROTEIN, 5 G NET CARBS.**

## Ingredients

- ✓ Seasoned salt, 1 tsp.
- ✓ 6 Eggs
- ✓ Chopped ham, .5 c
- ✓ Milk, .3 c
- ✓ Shredded mozzarella, .5 c

## Method

1. Begin by spraying four ramekins with cooking spray.

2. Set your air fryer to 350 °F and let it warm.

3. Place everything into a bowl and mix until well incorporated.

4. Divide evenly between the four ramekins.

5. Carefully place each ramekin into the fryer.

6. Cook for eight minutes.

7. Carefully remove each soufflé from the fryer and set aside to cool.

# Pizza Egg

**THE 4 SERVINGS CONTAIN: 284 CAL, 17 G FAT, 21 G PROTEIN, 7 G NET CARBS.**

## Ingredients

- ✓ Pepperoni slices, 4
- ✓ 2 Eggs
- ✓ Shredded mozzarella, 2 tbsp.
- ✓ Basil, .5 tsp.
- ✓ Oregano, .5 tsp.

## Method

1. Spray the ramekins with cooking spray.

2. Crack the eggs into a bowl. Toss in the basil and oregano. Mix to combine.

3. Pour the mixture into the ramekins.

4. Carefully place into the fryer.

5. Set your air fryer to 320°F and cook for three minutes.

6. Serve while hot.

# Spinach & Ham Frittata

**THE 4 SERVINGS CONTAIN: 191 CAL, 14 G FAT, 14 G PROTEIN, 2 G NET CARBS.**

## Ingredients

- ✓ 4 Eggs
- ✓ Chopped ham, 7 oz.
- ✓ Olive oil, 1 tbsp.
- ✓ Spinach, 2.25 c
- ✓ Whipping cream, 4 tsp.

## Method

1. Spray four ramekins with cooking spray.

2. Set your air fryer to 356°F.

3. Place a pan on medium heat and heat up the olive oil. Toss in the spinach and cook until wilted. Drain if necessary.

4. Divide the spinach evenly between the four ramekins.

5. Crack the eggs into a large bowl alongside the ham and whipping cream and season to your liking.

6. Whisk until everything is thoroughly combined. Divide evenly on top of the spinach.

7. Cook for 12 minutes. Serve hot!

# Egg Salad

**THE 4 SERVINGS CONTAIN: 163 CAL, 8.4 G FAT, 2 G PROTEIN, 2.68 G NET CARBS.**

## Ingredients

- ✓ Butter, 4 tbsp.
- ✓ Pepper and Salt
- ✓ 4 Eggs

## Method

1. Place the eggs into a baking dish of a size that will fit into your fryer.

2. Set your air fryer to 300°F. Place the baking dish into the fryer and cook for 18 minutes.

3. When cooked, place the eggs in ice water to chill. When cool, peel the eggs and place them into a bowl.

4. Mash them together with a fork alongside the butter, pepper, and salt until as smooth as you would like it.

5. Serve with your favorite bread.

# Scrambled Eggs & Crispy Bacon

**THE 2 SERVINGS CONTAIN: 446 CAL, 33.7 G FAT, 24.5 G PROTEIN, 1.3 G NET CARBS.**

## Ingredients

- ✓ Grated cheddar cheese, .5 c
- ✓ Melted unsalted butter, 2 tbsp.
- ✓ 4Eggs
- ✓ Sugar-free bacon, 4 slices

## Method

1. Place the bacon into the basket of your air fryer.

2. Set your air fryer to 400°F and cook for 12 minutes. When done, put to the side.

3. In a heat-safe baking dish, combine the eggs together with some pepper and salt. Carefully place the dish into the basket of your fryer.

4. Set the fryer to 400°F and cook for ten minutes.

5. At the 5-minute mark, toss in the cheese and butter. Mix well. Cook for three minutes more.

6. Cook the eggs for 2 more minutes. Remove them and fluff with a fork.

7. Divide them onto two plates and serve with two slices of crispy bacon.

# Hardboiled Eggs

**THE 4 SERVINGS CONTAIN: 78 CAL, 4.5 G FAT, 6.2 G PROTEIN, 0 G NET CARBS.**

## Ingredients
- ✓ Water, 1 c
- ✓ Eggs, 4

## Method
1. Place the eggs inside a 4-cup round dish the dish. Pour in the water. Carefully ease the dish into your fryer.

2. Set the fryer to 300°F and cook for 18 minutes.

3. Serve or store into a bag for later.

# Healthy Avocado "Toast"

**THE 2 SERVINGS CONTAIN: 277 CAL, 15.5 G FAT, 13.2 G PROTEIN, 7.6 G NET CARBS.**

## Ingredients
- ✓ Steamer bag of cauliflower, 12-oz
- ✓ Seasoned salt, .75 tsp.
- ✓ Ripe medium avocado
- ✓ Shredded mozzarella, .5 c
- ✓ 1 Egg

## Method
1. Cook the cauliflower and toss it inside a bowl. Mix in the mozzarella and egg.
2. Lay a piece of parchment paper inside your air fryer frying basket. Divide the cauliflower mixture in half and place it on the parchment in two mounds. Divide the cauliflower mixture into ¼-inch thick squares.
3. Set your fryer to 400°F and cook for eight minutes.
4. At the 4-minute mark, flip the cauliflower over to brown ir on both sides.
5. When done, carefully lift out of the frying basket using the parchment paper.
6. Cut open the avocado and remove the innards. Mash the innards (except the pip) in a bowl with the salt.
7. Spread the avocado across the cauliflower toast and enjoy.

# Buffalo Egg Cups

**THE 2 SERVINGS CONTAIN: 353 CAL, 21.3 G FAT, 20 G PROTEIN, 2.2 G NET CARBS.**

## Ingredients

- ✓ Grated cheddar cheese, .5 c
- ✓ Buffalo sauce, 2 tbsp.
- ✓ Whole-fat cream cheese, 2 oz.
- ✓ 4 Eggs

## Method

1. Break the two eggs into greased ramekins.

2. In a microwavable bowl, combine the cedar cheese, buffalo sauce and cream cheese. Microwave for 20 seconds. Stir everything together until well combined. Divide the mixture into each ramekin on top of the eggs.

3. Ease the ramekins into the basket of your air fryer.

4. Set your fryer to 320°F and cook for 15 minutes. When cooked, serve hot.

# Cheese & Sausage Balls

**THE 16 SERVINGS CONTAIN: 421 CAL, 34 G FAT, 21 G PROTEIN, 1.5 G NET CARBS.**

## Ingredients

- ✓ 1 Egg
- ✓ Softened full-fat cream cheese, 1 oz.
- ✓ Shredded cheddar cheese, .5 c
- ✓ Pork breakfast sausage, 1 lb.

## Method

1. Mix everything together in a bowl. Form into 16 1-inch sized sausage balls. Place the sausage balls into the basket of your air fryer.

2. Set your air fryer to 400°F and cook for 12 minutes.

3. During cooking, shake the cooking basket to prevent sticking.

4. Serve hot.

# Chicken Strips

**THE 4 SERVINGS CONTAIN: 244 CAL, 11.2 G FAT, 32 G PROTEIN, 0.5 G NET CARBS.**

## Ingredients

- ✓ Salt and Pepper
- ✓ Butter
- ✓ 1 lb. chicken fillet
- ✓ 1 tbsp. heavy whipping cream
- ✓ 1 tsp paprika

## Method

1. Using a clean scissors, cut the fillet into strips and season each one with salt and pepper to your taste.

2. Pre-heat your fryer to 365°F. Scoop some butter into the basket and wait until it has melted.

3. Add in the strips and cook them for six minutes, before turning them and cooking for a further five minutes.

4. In the meantime, mix together the paprika and heavy whipping cream.

5. Make sure the strips are cooked through, then dip each one into the cream-paprika mixture. Serve hot.

# Beef & Broccoli

**THE 4 SERVINGS CONTAIN: 186 CAL, 7.2 G FAT, 3.7 G PROTEIN, 3.7 G NET CARBS.**

## Ingredients

- ✓ ½ lb. beef brisket
- ✓ Salt and pepper to taste
- ✓ 1 cup broccoli, chopped
- ✓ 1 tsp. butter
- ✓ 1/3 cup water
- ✓ 1 onion, thinly sliced

## Method

6. Slice the brisket relatively thinly and season as desired.

7. Pre-heat your fryer at 360°F. Spritz the basket with the cooking spray.

8. Place the brisket in the tray and cook for seven minutes, stirring once.

9. Add in the broccoli, followed by the butter and water. Mix well.

10. Finally, add the sliced onion, and mix once more.

11. Bring the temperature down to 265°F and continue to cook for another six minutes. Serve hot and enjoy!

# Goulash

**THE 6 SERVINGS CONTAIN: 160 CAL, 6.2 G FAT, 20.5 G PROTEIN, 4.4 G NET CARBS.**

## Ingredients

- ✓ 2 chopped bell peppers
- ✓ 2 diced tomatoes
- ✓ 1 lb. ground chicken
- ✓ ½ cup chicken broth
- ✓ Salt and pepper

## Method

12. Pre-heat your fryer at 365°F and spray with cooking spray.

13. Cook the bell pepper for five minutes.

14. Add in the diced tomatoes and ground chicken. Combine well, then allow to cook for a further six minutes.

15. Pour in chicken broth, and season to taste with salt and pepper. Cook for another six minutes before serving.

# Mac & Cheese

**THE 4 SERVINGS CONTAIN: 144.5 CAL, 10.4 G FAT, 27 G PROTEIN, 1.3 G NET CARBS.**

## Ingredients

- ✓ 1 head cauliflower, chopped
- ✓ 3 tbsp. avocado oil
- ✓ ¼ cup unsweetened almond milk
- ✓ ¼ cup heavy cream
- ✓ 1 cup shredded cheddar cheese

## Method

1. Pre-heat your fryer to 400°F.

2. Drizzle some of the avocado oil over the cauliflower and toss, coating it entirely. Season to your taste.

3. Place the cauliflower in the fryer.

4. Add the rest of the avocado oil, milk, cream, and cheddar into a saucepan. Cook over a medium heat, stirring constantly, until the cheese has melted.

5. Pour over the cauliflower, then cook for fourteen minutes and serve hot.

# Ham Hash

**THE 3 SERVINGS CONTAIN: 371 CAL, 24.7 G FAT, 32.2 G PROTEIN, 5.8 G NET CARBS.**

## Ingredients

- ✓ 1 egg
- ✓ 1 cup ham, chopped
- ✓ ½ onion, chopped
- ✓ 1 tbsp. butter
- ✓ 1/3 cup parmesan, grated

## Method

1. Pre-heat your fryer to 350°F.

2. Crack the egg into a bowl and whisk well, before adding in the ham, onion, and butter. Combine well and add seasoning if desired.

3. Scoop equal portions into three ramekins, adding a sprinkle of parmesan on top.

4. Place into fryer and cook for ten minutes. Take care when removing the ramekins and serve hot.

# Meaty Egg Rolls

**THE 6 SERVINGS CONTAIN: 155 CAL, 9.4 G FAT, 12 G PROTEIN, 1.2 G NET CARBS.**

## Ingredients

- ✓ ¼ cup water
- ✓ ½ almond flour
- ✓ 1 tsp. salt
- ✓ ½ lb. ground beef

## Method

1. Pour water into a saucepan over medium heat and wait until it comes to a boil.

2. In a bowl, add in the almond flour and salt and pour the boiling water on top. Combine well, then knead with your fingers to form a soft dough. Then set aside.

3. Season the ground beef as desired, covering it evenly.

4. Put the beef into a skillet over medium heat. Cook until browned and drain if necessary. Crack in the egg and mix, then cook for an additional four minutes.

5. Roll out the dough with a pin and cut it into six equal-sized squares.

6. Spoon an equal amount of ground beef into the center of each square, and roll into cylinders.

7. Spray your fryer with cooking spray and pre-heat to 350°F. Cook the rolls for eight minutes and enjoy!

# Cheesy Meatballs

**THE 6 SERVINGS CONTAIN: 158 CAL, 9.5 G FAT, 19 G PROTEIN, 1.8 G NET CARBS.**

## Ingredients

- ✓ 1 cup minced onion
- ✓ 1 lb. ground beef
- ✓ 3 egg yolks
- ✓ 1 cup mozzarella, shredded
- ✓ 1 tbsp. extra virgin olive oil

## Method

1. Pre-heat your fryer at 375°F. Grease with the olive oil.

2. Put the onion and ground beef in a bowl and season as desired. Combine with the egg yolks with your hands.

3. Take a handful of beef and press it out flat with your palm. Place a small amount of cheese on the meat and wrap the meat around it, forming a ball. Repeat with the rest of the beef and cheese.

4. Put all of the meatballs in the fryer and cook for ten minutes. Serve hot.

# Sesame Chicken Wings

**THE 2 SERVINGS CONTAIN: 205 CAL, 17.9 G FAT, 6.1 G PROTEIN, 7 G NET CARBS.**

## Ingredients

- ✓ 2 lb. chicken wings
- ✓ 1 ½ tbsp. extra virgin olive oil
- ✓ 2 tbsp. dry rub
- ✓ ½ mayonnaise tbsp.
- ✓ 1 tbsp. sesame seeds

## Method

16. Pre-heat your fryer to 400°F.

17. Using a brush, coat the chicken wings with the olive oil, then cover with the dry rub of your choice. Leave to sit for five minutes.

18. Place the wings in the fryer. Cook for fifteen minutes.

19. When the wings are cooked through, place them on a serving platter and season with mayonnaise and sesame seeds if desired. Enjoy!

# Garlicky Chicken Meatballs

**THE 4 SERVINGS CONTAIN: 524 CAL, 45.7 G FAT, 22.6 G PROTEIN, 5.1 G NET CARBS.**

## Ingredients

- ✓ ½ lb. boneless chicken thighs
- ✓ 1 tsp. minced garlic
- ✓ 1 ¼ cup roasted pecans
- ✓ ½ cup mushrooms
- ✓ 1 tsp. extra virgin olive oil

## Method

1. Preheat your fryer to 375°F.

2. Cube the chicken thighs.

3. Place them in the food processor along with the garlic, pecans, and other seasonings as desired. Pulse until a smooth consistency is achieved.

4. Chop the mushrooms finely. Add to the chicken mixture and combine.

5. Using your hands, shape the mixture into balls and brush them with olive oil.

6. Put the balls into the fryer and cook for eighteen minutes. Serve hot.

# Cilantro Drumsticks

**THE 8 SERVINGS CONTAIN: 395 CAL, 36.1 G FAT, 17.3 G PROTEIN, 1.5 G NET CARBS.**

## Ingredients

- ✓ 8 chicken drumsticks
- ✓ ½ cup chimichurri sauce
- ✓ ¼ cup lemon juice

## Method

1. Coat the chicken drumsticks with chimichurri sauce and refrigerate in an airtight container for no less than an hour, ideally overnight.

2. When it's time to cook, pre-heat your fryer to 400°F.

3. Remove the chicken from refrigerator and allow return to room temperature for roughly twenty minutes.

4. Cook for eighteen minutes in the fryer. Drizzle with lemon juice to taste and enjoy.

# Pop Corn Chicken

**THE 5 SERVINGS CONTAIN: 146 CAL, 5.7 G FAT, 14 G PROTEIN, 3.6 G NET CARBS.**

## Ingredients

- ✓ 1 lb. skinless, boneless chicken breast
- ✓ 1 tsp. chili flakes
- ✓ 1 tsp. garlic powder
- ✓ ½ cup coconut flour
- ✓ 1 tbsp. olive oil cooking spray

## Method

1. Pre-heat your fryer at 365°F. Spray with olive oil.

2. Cut the chicken breasts into cubes and place in a bowl. Toss with the chili flakes, garlic powder, and additional seasonings to taste and make sure to coat entirely.

3. Add the coconut flour and toss once more.

4. Cook the chicken in the fryer for ten minutes. Turn over and cook for a further five minutes before serving.

# Crispy Chicken Skins

**THE 6 SERVINGS CONTAIN: 351 CAL, 32.4 G FAT, 14.5 G PROTEIN, .2 G NET CARBS.**

## Ingredients

- ✓ 1 lb. chicken skin
- ✓ 1 tsp. butter
- ✓ ½ tsp. chili flakes
- ✓ 1 tsp. dill

## Method

1. Pre-heat the fryer at 360°F.

2. Cut the chicken skin into slices.

3. Heat the butter until melted and pour it over the chicken skin. Toss with chili flakes, dill, and any additional seasonings to taste, making sure to coat well.

4. Cook the skins in the fryer for three minutes. Turn them over and cook on the other side for another three minutes.

5. Serve immediately or save them for later – they can be eaten hot or at room temperature.

# POULTRY

# Southern Fried Chicken

**THE 4 SERVINGS CONTAIN: 193 CAL, 6.8 G FAT, 28.8 G PROTEIN, 2 G NET CARBS.**

## Ingredients

- ✓ 2 x 6-oz. boneless skinless chicken breasts
- ✓ 2 tbsp. hot sauce
- ✓ ½ tsp. onion powder
- ✓ 1 tbsp. chili powder
- ✓ 2 oz. pork rinds, finely ground

## Method

1. Cut the chicken breasts in half lengthwise and rub in the hot sauce. Combine the onion powder with the chili powder, then rub into the chicken. Leave to marinate for at least a half hour.

2. Use the ground pork rinds to coat the chicken breasts in the ground pork rinds, covering them thoroughly. Place the chicken in your fryer.

3. Set the fryer at 350°F and cook the chicken for 13 minutes. Flip the chicken and cook the other side for another 13 minutes or until golden.

4. Test the chicken with a meat thermometer. When fully cooked, it should reach 165°F. Serve hot, with the sides of your choice.

# Jalapeno Chicken Breast

**THE 2 SERVINGS CONTAIN: 505 CAL, 24.3 G FAT, 54.8 G PROTEIN, 1.3 G NET CARBS.**

## Ingredients

- ✓ 2 oz. full-fat cream cheese, softened
- ✓ 4 slices sugar-free bacon, cooked and crumbled
- ✓ ¼ cup pickled jalapenos, sliced
- ✓ ½ cup sharp cheddar cheese, shredded and divided
- ✓ 2 x 6-oz. boneless skinless chicken breasts

## Method

1. In a bowl, mix the cream cheese, bacon, jalapeno slices, and half of the cheddar cheese until well-combined.

2. Cut parallel slits in the chicken breasts of about ¾ the length – make sure not to cut all the way down. You should be able to make between six and eight slices, depending on the size of the chicken breast.

3. Insert evenly sized dollops of the cheese mixture into the slits of the chicken breasts. Top the chicken with sprinkles of the rest of the cheddar cheese. Place the chicken in the basket of your air fryer.

4. Set the fryer to 350°F and cook the chicken breasts for twenty minutes.

5. Test with a meat thermometer. The chicken should be at 165°F when fully cooked. Serve hot and enjoy!

# Fajita Style Chicken Breast

**THE 4 SERVINGS CONTAIN: 145 CAL, 4.8 G FAT, 17.8 G PROTEIN, 2 G NET CARBS.**

## Ingredients

- ✓ 2 x 6-oz. boneless skinless chicken breasts
- ✓ 1 green bell pepper, sliced
- ✓ ¼ medium white onion, sliced
- ✓ 1 tbsp. coconut oil, melted
- ✓ 3 tsp. taco seasoning mix

## Method

1. Cut each chicken breast in half and place each one between two sheets of cooking parchment. Using a mallet, pound the chicken to flatten to a quarter-inch thick.

2. Place the chicken on a flat surface, with the short end facing you. Place four slices of pepper and three slices of onion at the end of each piece of chicken. Roll up the chicken tightly, making sure not to let any veggies fall out. Secure with some toothpicks or with butcher's string.

3. Coat the chicken with coconut oil and then with taco seasoning. Place into your air fryer.

4. Turn the fryer to 350°F and cook the chicken for twenty-five minutes.

5. Serve the rolls immediately with your favorite dips and sides.

# Lemon Pepper Chicken Legs

**THE 4 SERVINGS CONTAIN: 535 CAL, 34.3 G FAT, 49.3 G PROTEIN, 1.5 G NET CARBS.**

## Ingredients

- ✓ ½ tsp. garlic powder
- ✓ 2 tsp. baking powder
- ✓ 8 chicken legs
- ✓ 4 tbsp. salted butter, melted
- ✓ 1 tbsp. lemon pepper seasoning

## Method

1. In a small bowl combine the garlic powder and baking powder, then use this mixture to coat the chicken legs. Lay the chicken in the basket of your fryer.

2. Cook the chicken legs at 375°F for twenty-five minutes. Halfway through, turn them over and allow to cook on the other side.

3. When the chicken has turned golden brown, test with a thermometer to ensure it has reached an ideal temperature of 165°F. Remove from the fryer.

4. Mix together the melted butter and lemon pepper seasoning and toss with the chicken legs until the chicken is coated all over. Serve hot.

# Greek Chicken Meatballs

**THE 4 SERVINGS CONTAIN: 225 CAL, 11.5 G FAT, 26.1 G PROTEIN, 1.5 G NET CARBS.**

## Ingredients

- ½ oz. finely ground pork rinds
- 1 lb. ground chicken
- 1 tsp. Greek seasoning
- 1/3 cup feta, crumbled
- 1/3 cup frozen spinach, drained and thawed

## Method

1. Place all the ingredients in a large bowl, and combine using your hands. Take equal-sized portions of this mixture and roll each into a 2-inch ball. Place the balls in your fryer.

2. Cook the meatballs at 350°F for twelve minutes, in several batches if necessary.

3. Once they are golden, ensure they have reached an ideal temperature of 165°F and remove from the fryer. Keep each batch warm while you move on to the next one. Serve with Tzatziki if desired.

# Almond-Crusted Chicken

**THE 4 SERVINGS CONTAIN: 197 CAL, 11.5 G FAT, 21.8 G PROTEIN, 1 G NET CARBS.**

## Ingredients

- ¼ cup slivered almonds
- 2x 6-oz. boneless skinless chicken breasts
- 2 tbsp. full-fat mayonnaise
- 1 tbsp. Dijon mustard

## Method

1. Pulse the almonds in a food processor until they are finely chopped. Spread the almonds on a plate and set aside.

2. Cut each chicken breast in half lengthwise.

3. Mix the mayonnaise and mustard together and then spread evenly on top of the chicken slices.

4. Place the chicken into the plate of chopped almonds to coat completely, laying each coated slice into the basket of your fryer.

5. Cook for 25 minutes at 350°F until golden. Test the temperature, making sure the chicken has reached 165°F. Serve hot.

# Cheesy Buffalo Chicken Tenders

**THE 2 SERVINGS CONTAIN: 365 CAL, 20.4 G FAT, 36.8 G PROTEIN, 3 G NET CARBS.**

## Ingredients

- ✓ 1 egg
- ✓ 1 cup mozzarella cheese, shredded
- ✓ ¼ cup buffalo sauce
- ✓ 1 cup cooked chicken, shredded
- ✓ ¼ cup feta cheese

## Method

1. Combine together all ingredients (except for the feta). Line the basket of your fryer with a suitably sized piece of parchment paper. Lay the mixture into the fryer and press it into a circle about half an inch thick. Crumble the feta cheese over it.

2. Cook for eight minutes at 400°F. Turn the fryer off and allow the chicken to rest inside before removing with care.

3. Cut the mixture into slices and serve hot.

# Crunchy Buffalo Chicken Strips

**THE 4 SERVINGS CONTAIN: 165 CAL, 4.7 G FAT, 26.3 G PROTEIN, 1.5 G NET CARBS.**

## Ingredients

- ✓ ¼ cup hot sauce
- ✓ 1 lb. boneless skinless chicken tenders
- ✓ 1 tsp. garlic powder
- ✓ 1 ½ oz. pork rinds, finely ground
- ✓ 1 tsp chili powder

## Method

1. Toss the hot sauce and chicken tenders together in a bowl, ensuring the chicken is completely coated.

2. In another bowl, combine the garlic powder, ground pork rinds, and chili powder. Use this mixture to coat the tenders, covering them well. Place the chicken into your fryer, taking care not to layer pieces on top of one another.

3. Cook the chicken at 375°F for twenty minutes until cooked all the way through and golden. Serve warm with your favorite dips and sides.

# Chicken and Pepperoni Pizza

**THE 4 SERVINGS CONTAIN: 355 CAL, 18.5 G FAT, 33.2 G PROTEIN, 5.4 G NET CARBS.**

## Ingredients

- ✓ 2 cups cooked chicken, cubed
- ✓ 20 slices pepperoni
- ✓ 1 cup sugar-free pizza sauce
- ✓ 1 cup mozzarella cheese, shredded
- ✓ ¼ cup parmesan cheese, grated

## Method

1. Place the chicken into the base of a four-cup baking dish and add the pepperoni and pizza sauce on top. Mix well so as to completely coat the meat with the sauce.

2. Add the parmesan and mozzarella on top of the chicken, then place the baking dish into your fryer.

3. Cook for 15 minutes at 375°F.

4. When everything is bubbling and melted, remove from the fryer. Serve hot.

# Italian Chicken Thighs

**THE 2 SERVINGS CONTAIN: 595 CAL, 31.8 G FAT, 67.2 G PROTEIN, 1 G NET CARBS.**

## Ingredients

- ✓ skin-on bone-in chicken thighs
- ✓ 2 tbsp. unsalted butter, melted
- ✓ 3 tsp. Italian herbs
- ✓ ½ tsp. garlic powder
- ✓ ¼ tsp. onion powder

## Method

1. Using a brush, coat the chicken thighs with the melted butter. Combine the herbs with the garlic powder and onion powder, then massage into the chicken thighs. Place the thighs in the fryer.

2. Cook at 380°F for 20 minutes, turning the chicken halfway through to cook on the other side.

3. When the thighs have achieved a golden color, test the temperature with a meat thermometer. Once they have reached 165°F, remove from the fryer and serve.

# Teriyaki Chicken Wings

**THE 4 SERVINGS CONTAIN: 436 CAL, 28.7 G FAT, 42.7 G PROTEIN, 2 G NET CARBS.**

## Ingredients

- ¼ tsp. ground ginger
- 2 tsp. minced garlic
- ½ cup sugar-free teriyaki sauce
- 2 lb. chicken wings
- 2 tsp. baking powder

## Method

1. In a small bowl, combine together the ginger, garlic, and teriyaki sauce. Place the chicken wings in a separate, larger bowl and pour the mixture over them. Toss to coat until the chicken is well covered.

2. Refrigerate for at least an hour.

3. Remove the marinated wings from the fridge and add the baking powder, tossing again to coat. Then place the chicken in the basket of your air fryer.

4. Cook for 25 minutes at 400°F, giving the basket a shake intermittently throughout the cooking time.

5. When the wings are 165°F and golden in color, remove from the fryer and serve immediately.

# Chicken Pizza Crust

**THE 4 SERVINGS CONTAIN: 235 CAL, 11.8 G FAT, 25.7 G PROTEIN, 1.5 G NET CARBS.**

## Ingredients

- ½ cup mozzarella, shredded
- ¼ cup parmesan cheese, grated
- 1 lb. ground chicken

## Method

1. In a large bowl, combine all the ingredients and then spread the mixture out, dividing it into four parts of equal size.

2. Cut a sheet of parchment paper into four circles, roughly six inches in diameter, and put some of the chicken mixture onto the center of each piece, flattening the mixture to fill out the circle.

3. Depending on the size of your fryer, cook either one or two circles at a time at 375°F for 25 minutes. Halfway through, turn the crust over to cook on the other side. Keep each batch warm while you move onto the next one.

4. Once all the crusts are cooked, top with cheese and the toppings of your choice. If desired, cook the topped crusts for an additional five minutes.

5. Serve hot, or freeze and save for later!

# Crispy Chicken Thighs

**THE 8 SERVINGS CONTAIN: 456 CAL, 42.7 G FAT, 17 G PROTEIN, 6.2 G NET CARBS.**

## Ingredients

- ✓ 1 lb. chicken thighs
- ✓ Salt and pepper
- ✓ 2 cups roasted pecans
- ✓ 1 cup water
- ✓ 1 cup almond flour

## Method

1. Pre-heat your fryer to 400°F.

2. Season the chicken with salt and pepper, then set aside.

3. Pulse the roasted pecans in a food processor until a flour-like consistency is achieved.

4. Fill a dish with the water, another with the almond flour, and a third with the pecans.

5. Coat the thighs with the almond flour. Mix the remaining flour with the processed pecans.

6. Dredge the thighs in the water and then press into the almond-pecan mix, ensuring the chicken is completely covered.

7. Cook the chicken in the fryer for twenty-two minutes, with an extra five minutes added if you would like the chicken a darker-brown color. Check the temperature has reached 165°F before serving.

# Strawberry Turkey

**THE 4 SERVINGS CONTAIN: 334 CAL, 27.3 G FAT, 16.7 G PROTEIN, 7.7 G NET CARBS.**

## Ingredients

- ✓ 2 lb. turkey breast
- ✓ 1 tbsp. olive oil
- ✓ Salt and pepper
- ✓ 1 cup fresh strawberries

## Method

1. Pre-heat your fryer to 375°F.

2. Massage the turkey breast with olive oil, before seasoning with a generous amount of salt and pepper.

3. Cook the turkey in the fryer for fifteen minutes. Flip the turkey and cook for a further fifteen minutes.

4. During these last fifteen minutes, blend the strawberries in a food processor until a smooth consistency has been achieved.

5. Heap the strawberries over the turkey, then cook for a final seven minutes and enjoy.

# Chimichurri Turkey

**THE 4 SERVINGS CONTAIN: 405 CAL, 35.3 G FAT, 15.8 G PROTEIN, 4.5 G NET CARBS.**

## Ingredients

- ✓ 1 lb. turkey breast
- ✓ ½ cup chimichurri sauce
- ✓ ½ cup butter
- ✓ ¼ cup parmesan cheese, grated
- ✓ ¼ tsp. garlic powder

## Method

1. Massage the chimichurri sauce into the turkey breast, then refrigerate in an airtight container for at least a half hour.

2. In the meantime, prepare the herbed butter. Mix together the butter, parmesan, and garlic powder, using a hand mixer if desired (this will make it extra creamy)

3. Preheat your fryer at 350°F and place a rack inside. Remove the turkey from the refrigerator and allow to return to room temperature for roughly twenty minutes while the fryer warms.

4. Place the turkey in the fryer and allow to cook for twenty minutes. Flip and cook on the other side for a further twenty minutes.

5. Take care when removing the turkey from the fryer. Place it on a serving dish and enjoy with the herbed butter.

# Baked Chicken

**THE 4 SERVINGS CONTAIN: 277 CAL, 28.6 G FAT, 5.4 G PROTEIN, 2.3 G NET CARBS.**

## Ingredients

- ✓ ½ cup butter
- ✓ 1 tsp. pepper
- ✓ 3 tbsp. garlic, minced
- ✓ 1 whole chicken

## Method

1. Pre-heat your fryer at 350°F.

2. Allow the butter to soften at room temperature, then mix well in a small bowl with the pepper and garlic.

3. Massage the butter into the chicken. Any remaining butter can go inside the chicken.

4. Cook the chicken in the fryer for half an hour. Flip, then cook on the other side for an another thirty minutes.

5. Test the temperature of the chicken by sticking a meat thermometer into the fat of the thigh to make sure it has reached 165°F. Take care when removing the chicken from the fryer. Let sit for ten minutes before you carve it and serve.

# Chicken Breasts & Spiced Tomatoes

**THE 8 SERVINGS CONTAIN: 365 CAL, 31 G FAT, 17.1 G PROTEIN, 1 G NET CARBS.**

## Ingredients

- ✓ 1 lb. boneless chicken breast
- ✓ Salt and pepper
- ✓ 1 cup butter
- ✓ 1 cup tomatoes, diced
- ✓ 1 ½ tsp. paprika
- ✓ 1 tsp. pumpkin pie spices

## Method

1. Preheat your fryer at 375°F.

2. Cut the chicken into relatively thick slices and put them in the fryer. Sprinkle with salt and pepper to taste. Cook for fifteen minutes.

3. In the meantime, melt the butter in a saucepan over medium heat, before adding the tomatoes, paprika, and pumpkin pie spices. Leave simmering while the chicken finishes cooking.

4. When the chicken is cooked through, place it on a dish and pour the tomato mixture over. Serve hot.

# Fennel Chicken

**THE 4 SERVINGS CONTAIN: 418 CAL, 35.7 G FAT, 21.5 G PROTEIN, 6.5 G NET CARBS.**

## Ingredients

- ✓ 1 ½ cup coconut milk
- ✓ 2 tbsp. garam masala
- ✓ 1 ½ lb. chicken thighs
- ✓ ¾ tbsp. coconut oil, melted

## Method

1. Combine the coconut oil and garam masala together in a bowl. Pour the mixture over the chicken thighs and leave to marinate for a half hour.

2. Pre-heat your fryer at 375°F .

3. Cook the chicken into the fryer for fifteen minutes.

4. Add in the coconut milk, giving it a good stir, then cook for an additional ten minutes.

5. Remove the chicken and place on a serving dish. Make sure to pour all of the coconut "gravy" over it and serve immediately.

# Roasted Chicken

**THE 12 SERVINGS CONTAIN: 455 CAL, 21.1 G FAT, 64.6 G PROTEIN, .7 G NET CARBS.**

## Ingredients

- ✓ lb. whole chicken
- ✓ 1 tsp. olive oil
- ✓ 1 tbsp. minced garlic
- ✓ 1 white onion, peeled and halved
- ✓ 3 tbsp. butter

## Method

1. Pre-heat the fryer at 360°F.

2. Massage the chicken with the olive oil and the minced garlic.

3. Place the peeled and halved onion, as well as the butter, inside of the chicken.

4. Cook the chicken in the fryer for seventy-five minutes.

5. Take care when removing the chicken from the fryer, then carve and serve.

# BEEF, PORK & LAMB

# Breaded Pork Chops

**THE 4 SERVINGS CONTAIN: 272 CAL, 17.5 G FAT, 28.5 G PROTEIN, 0 G NET CARBS.**

## Ingredients

- ✓ 1 tsp. chili powder
- ✓ ½ tsp. garlic powder
- ✓ 1 ½ oz. pork rinds, finely ground
- ✓ 4 x 4-oz. pork chops
- ✓ 1 tbsp. coconut oil, melted

## Method

1. Combine the chili powder, garlic powder, and ground pork rinds.

2. Coat the pork chops with the coconut oil, followed by the pork rind mixture, taking care to cover them completely. Then place the chops in the basket of the fryer.

3. Cook the chops for fifteen minutes at 400°F, turning halfway through.

4. Once they are browned, check the temperature has reached 145°F before serving with the sides of your choice.

# Pulled Pork

**THE 8 SERVINGS CONTAIN: 536 CAL, 34.5 G FAT, 42.6 G PROTEIN, 0 G NET CARBS.**

## Ingredients

- ✓ 1 tsp. garlic powder
- ✓ ½ tsp. cumin
- ✓ ½ tsp. onion powder
- ✓ 2 tbsp. chili powder
- ✓ 4 lb. pork shoulder

## Method

1. Combine all of the seasonings in a bowl, adding in some salt and pepper if desired. Coat the pork shoulder with the seasonings and place it into the fryer.

2. Cook at 350°F for two hours and twenty minutes.

3. When the pork is ready, the skin should be crispy and the meat should be falling off the bone. Check the temperature has reached 145°F with a meat thermometer. Then shred the meat and serve with the sauces and sides of your choice.

# Juicy Mexican Pork Chops

**THE 2 SERVINGS CONTAIN: 311 CAL, 25.6 G FAT, 22.4 G PROTEIN, 0.5 G NET CARBS.**

## Ingredients

- ✓ ¼ tsp. dried oregano
- ✓ 1 ½ tsp. taco seasoning mix
- ✓ 2 x 4-oz. boneless pork chops
- ✓ 2 tbsp. unsalted butter, divided

## Method

1. Combine the dried oregano and taco seasoning to rub into the pork chops.

2. In your fryer, cook the chops at 400°F for fifteen minutes, turning them over halfway through to cook on the other side.

3. When the chops are a brown color, check the internal temperature has reached 145°F and remove from the fryer. Serve with a garnish of butter.

# Baby Back Ribs

**THE 2 SERVINGS CONTAIN: 420 CAL, 33.7 G FAT, 12.9 G PROTEIN, 6.2 G NET CARBS.**

## Ingredients

- ✓ 2 tsp. red pepper flakes
- ✓ ¾ ground ginger
- ✓ 3 cloves minced garlic
- ✓ Salt and pepper
- ✓ 2 baby back ribs

## Method

1. Pre-heat your fryer at 350°F.

2. Combine the red pepper flakes, ginger, garlic, salt and pepper in a bowl, making sure to mix well. Massage the mixture into the baby back ribs.

3. Cook the ribs in the fryer for thirty minutes.

4. Take care when taking the rubs out of the fryer. Place them on a serving dish and enjoy with a low-carb barbecue sauce of your choosing.

# Pulled Pork

**THE 4 SERVINGS CONTAIN: 197 CAL, 6.5 G FAT, 30.8 G PROTEIN, 1.7 G NET CARBS.**

## Ingredients

- ✓ 1 lb. pork tenderloin
- ✓ 2 tbsp. barbecue dry rub
- ✓ 1/3 cup heavy cream
- ✓ 1 tsp. butter

## Method

1. Pre-heat your fryer at 370°F.

2. Massage the dry rub of your choice into the tenderloin, coating it well.

3. Cook the tenderloin in the fryer for twenty minutes. When cooked, shred with two forks.

4. Add the heavy cream and butter into the fryer along with the shredded pork and stir well. Cook for a further four minutes.

5. Allow to cool a little, then serve and enjoy.

# Ribs

**THE 5 SERVINGS CONTAIN: 264 CAL, 14.4 G FAT, 27.5 G PROTEIN, .5 G NET CARBS.**

## Ingredients

- ✓ 1 lb. pork ribs
- ✓ 1 tbsp. barbecue dry rub
- ✓ 1 tsp. mustard
- ✓ 1 tbsp. apple cider vinegar
- ✓ 1 tsp. sesame oil

## Method

1. Chop up the pork ribs.

2. Combine the dry rub, mustard, apple cider vinegar, and sesame oil, then coat the ribs with this mixture. Refrigerate the ribs for twenty minutes.

3. Preheat the fryer at 360°F.

4. When the ribs are ready, place them in the fryer and cook for 15 minutes. Flip them and cook on the other side for a further fifteen minutes. Then serve and enjoy!

# Pork Chops

**THE 3 SERVINGS CONTAIN: 415 CAL, 32.4 G FAT, 25.8 G PROTEIN, .5 G NET CARBS.**

## Ingredients

- ✓ 3 pork chops
- ✓ ½ tsp. dried rosemary
- ✓ 1 tsp. garlic salt
- ✓ 1 tsp. peppercorns
- ✓ 1 tbsp. butter

## Method

1. Pre-heat your fryer to 365°F.

2. Combine the dried rosemary and garlic salt, and rub into the pork chops.

3. Place the peppercorns and butter into the fryer and allow the butter to melt.

4. Add in the pork chops and cook for six minutes. Flip them and cook for an additional five minutes before serving.

# Taco Stuffed Peppers

**THE 4 SERVINGS CONTAIN: 310 CAL, 15.1 G FAT, 28.8 G PROTEIN, 2 G NET CARBS.**

## Ingredients

- ✓ 1 lb. ground beef
- ✓ 1 tbsp. taco seasoning mix
- ✓ 1 can diced tomatoes and green chilis
- ✓ 4 green bell peppers
- ✓ 1 cup shredded Monterey jack cheese, divided

## Method

1. Set a skillet over a high heat and cook the ground beef for seven to ten minutes. Make sure it is cooked through and brown all over. Drain the fat.

2. Stir in the taco seasoning mix, as well as the diced tomatoes and green chilis. Allow the mixture to cook for a further three to five minutes.

3. In the meantime, slice the tops off the green peppers and remove the seeds and membranes.

4. When the meat mixture is fully cooked, spoon equal amounts of it into the peppers and top with the Monterey jack cheese. Then place the peppers into your fryer.

5. Cook at 350°F for fifteen minutes.

6. The peppers are ready when they are soft and the cheese is bubbling and brown. Serve warm and enjoy!

# Beef Tenderloin & Peppercorn Crust

**THE 6 SERVINGS CONTAIN: 289 CAL, 13.8 G FAT, 34.7 G PROTEIN, 1 G NET CARBS.**

## Ingredients

- ✓ 2 lb. beef tenderloin
- ✓ 2 tsp. roasted garlic, minced
- ✓ 2 tbsp. salted butter, melted
- ✓ 3 tbsp. ground 4-peppercorn blender

## Method

1. Remove any surplus fat from the beef tenderloin.

2. Combine the roasted garlic and melted butter to apply to your tenderloin with a brush.

3. On a plate, spread out the peppercorns and roll the tenderloin in them, making sure they are covering and clinging to the meat.

4. Cook the tenderloin in your fryer for twenty-five minutes at 400°F, turning halfway through cooking.

5. Let the tenderloin rest for ten minutes before slicing and serving.

# Bratwursts

**THE 4 SERVINGS CONTAIN: 286 CAL, 24.8 G FAT, 11.8 G PROTEIN, 0 G NET CARBS.**

## Ingredients

- ✓ x 3-oz. beef bratwursts

## Method

1. Place the beef bratwursts in the basket of your fryer and cook for fifteen minutes at 375°F, turning once halfway through.

2. Enjoy with the low-carb toppings and sides of your choice.

# Bacon-Wrapped Hot Dog

**THE 4 SERVINGS CONTAIN: 197 CAL, 14 G FAT, 9.3 G PROTEIN, 1.2 G NET CARBS.**

## Ingredients

- ✓ slices sugar-free bacon
- ✓ 4 beef hot dogs

## Method

1. Take a slice of bacon and wrap it around the hot dog, securing it with a toothpick. Repeat with the other pieces of bacon and hot dogs, placing each wrapped dog in the basket of your fryer.

2. Cook at 370°F for ten minutes, turning halfway through to fry the other side.

3. Once hot and crispy, the hot dogs are ready to serve. Enjoy!

# Herb Shredded Beef

**THE 8 SERVINGS CONTAIN: 266 CAL, 15 G FAT, 31.4 G PROTEIN, 1 G NET CARBS.**

## Ingredients

- ✓ 1 tsp. dried dill
- ✓ 1 tsp. dried thyme
- ✓ 1 tsp. garlic powder
- ✓ 2 lbs. beefsteak
- ✓ 3 tbsp. butter

## Method

1. Pre-heat your fryer at 360°F.

2. Combine the dill, thyme, and garlic powder together, and massage into the steak.

3. Cook the steak in the fryer for twenty minutes, then remove, shred, and return to the fryer. Add the butter and cook for a further two minutes at 365°F. Make sure the beef is coated in the butter before serving.

# Herbed Butter Rib Eye Steak

**THE 4 SERVINGS CONTAIN: 431 CAL, 42.8 G FAT, 10.5 G PROTEIN, 4.2 G NET CARBS.**

## Ingredients

- ✓ ribeye steaks
- ✓ Olive oil
- ✓ ¾ tsp. dry rub
- ✓ ½ cup butter
- ✓ 1 tsp. dried basil
- ✓ 3 tbsp. lemon garlic seasoning

## Method

1. Massage the olive oil into the steaks and your favorite dry rub. Leave aside to sit for thirty minutes.

2. In a bowl, combine the button, dried basil, and lemon garlic seasoning, then refrigerate.

3. Pre-heat the fryer at 450°F and set a rack inside. Place the steaks on top of the rack and allow to cook for fifteen minutes.

4. Remove the steaks from the fryer when cooked and serve with the herbed butter.

# Flank Steak with Avocado Butter

**THE 2 SERVINGS CONTAIN: 315 CAL, 17.6 G FAT, 25.9 G PROTEIN, 2.8 G NET CARBS.**

## Ingredients

- ✓ 1 flank steak
- ✓ Salt and pepper
- ✓ 2 avocados
- ✓ 2 tbsp. butter, melted
- ✓ ½ cup chimichurri sauce

## Method

1. Rub the flank steak with salt and pepper to taste and leave to sit for twenty minutes.

2. Pre-heat the fryer at 400°F and place a rack inside.

3. Halve the avocados and take out the pits. Spoon the flesh into a bowl and mash with a fork. Mix in the melted butter and chimichurri sauce, making sure everything is well combined.

4. Put the steak in the fryer and cook for six minutes. Flip over and allow to cook for another six minutes.

5. Serve the steak with the avocado butter and enjoy!

# Mozzarella Beef

**THE 4 SERVINGS CONTAIN: 345 CAL, 17 G FAT, 41.1 G PROTEIN, 4.5 G NET CARBS.**

## Ingredients

- ✓ 12 oz. beef brisket
- ✓ 2 tsp. Italian herbs
- ✓ 2 tsp. butter
- ✓ 1 onion, sliced
- ✓ 7 oz. mozzarella cheese, sliced

## Method

1. Pre-heat the fryer at 365°F.

2. Cut up the brisket into four equal slices and season with the Italian herbs.

3. Allow the butter to melt in the fryer. Place the slices of beef inside along with the onion. Put a piece of mozzarella on top of each piece of brisket and cook for twenty-five minutes.

4. Enjoy!

# Rosemary Rib Eye Steaks

**THE 2 SERVINGS CONTAIN: 534 CAL, 48.2 G FAT, 21.8 G PROTEIN, 5 G NET CARBS.**

## Ingredients

- ✓ ¼ cup butter
- ✓ 1 clove minced garlic
- ✓ Salt and pepper
- ✓ 1 ½ tbsp. balsamic vinegar
- ✓ ¼ cup rosemary, chopped
- ✓ 2 ribeye steaks

## Method

1. Melt the butter in a skillet over medium heat. Add the garlic and fry until fragrant.

2. Remove the skillet from the heat and add in the salt, pepper, and vinegar. Allow it to cool.

3. Add the rosemary, then pour the whole mixture into a Ziploc bag.

4. Put the ribeye steaks in the bag and shake well, making sure to coat the meat well. Refrigerate for an hour, then allow to sit for a further twenty minutes.

5. Pre-heat the fryer at 400°F and set the rack inside. Cook the ribeyes for fifteen minutes.

6. Take care when removing the steaks from the fryer and plate up. Enjoy!

# Meatloaf

**THE 8 SERVINGS CONTAIN: 245 CAL, 17.3 G FAT, 14.7 G PROTEIN, 3.2 G NET CARBS.**

## Ingredients

- ✓ 1 egg
- ✓ 1 lb. ground beef
- ✓ 1 cup cheddar cheese, shredded
- ✓ ¼ cup chopped onion
- ✓ ½ cup tomato purée

## Method

1. Break the egg into a bowl, add desired seasoning, and whisk well with a fork.

2. Add the ground beef, cheese, and onion to the bowl, combining everything with your hands to make sure every thing is well-incorporated.

3. Put the mixture in a silicon loaf pan, pressing down on the top to ensure it is even. Pour the tomato purée over the top, then set the pan aside.

4. Pre-heat the fryer at 350°F. Cook the mixture for twenty minutes.

5. Take care when taking the pan out of the fryer, and let it cool for a few minutes before serving.

# Herbed Butter Beef Loin

**THE 3 SERVINGS CONTAIN: 444 CAL, 37.4 G FAT, 16.7 G PROTEIN, 5.5 G NET CARBS.**

## Ingredients

- ✓ 1 tbsp. butter, melted
- ✓ ¼ dried thyme
- ✓ 1 tsp. garlic salt
- ✓ ¼ tsp. dried parsley
- ✓ 1 lb. beef loin

## Method

1. In a bowl, combine the melted butter, thyme, garlic salt, and parsley.

2. Cut the beef loin into slices and generously apply the seasoned butter using a brush.

3. Pre-heat your fryer at 400°F and place a rack inside.

4. Cook the beef for fifteen minutes.

5. Take care when removing it, and serve hot.

# Lamb Ribs

**THE 1 SERVING CONTAINS: 162 CAL, 16.3 G FAT, 13.3 G PROTEIN, 4.1 G NET CARBS.**

## Ingredients

- ✓ 1 lb. lamb ribs
- ✓ 2 tbsp. mustard
- ✓ 1 tsp. rosemary, chopped
- ✓ Salt and pepper
- ✓ ¼ cup mint leaves, chopped
- ✓ 1 cup Green yogurt

## Method

1. Pre-heat the fryer at 350°F.

2. Use a brush to apply the mustard to the lamb ribs, and season with rosemary, as well as salt and pepper as desired.

3. Cook the ribs in the fryer for eighteen minutes.

4. Meanwhile, combine together the mint leaves and yogurt in a bowl.

5. Remove the lamb ribs from the fryer when cooked and serve with the mint yogurt. Enjoy!

# Lamb Satay

**THE 3 SERVINGS CONTAIN: 239 CAL, 21.2 G FAT, 13.9 G PROTEIN, 3.5 G NET CARBS.**

## Ingredients

- ✓ ¼ tsp. cumin
- ✓ 1 tsp ginger
- ✓ ½ tsp. nutmeg
- ✓ Salt and pepper
- ✓ 2 boneless lamb steaks
- ✓ Olive oil cooking spray

## Method

1. Combine the cumin, ginger, nutmeg, salt and pepper in a bowl.

2. Cube the lamb steaks and massage the spice mixture into each one.

3. Leave to marinate for ten minutes, then transfer onto metal skewers.

4. Pre-heat the fryer at 400°F.

5. Spritz the skewers with the olive oil cooking spray, then cook them in the fryer for eight minutes.

6. Take care when removing them from the fryer, and serve with the low-carb sauce of your choice.

# Italian Lamb Chops

**THE 2 SERVINGS CONTAIN: 368 CAL, 34.6 G FAT, 12.5 G PROTEIN, 9 G NET CARBS.**

## Ingredients

- ✓ 2 lamp chops
- ✓ 2 tsp. Italian herbs
- ✓ 2 avocados
- ✓ ½ cup mayonnaise
- ✓ 1 tbsp. lemon juice

## Method

1. Season the lamb chops with the Italian herbs, then set aside for five minutes.

2. Pre-heat the fryer at 400°F and place the rack inside.

3. Put the chops on the rack and allow to cook for twelve minutes.

4. In the meantime, halve the avocados and open to remove the pits. Spoon the flesh into a blender.

5. Add in the mayonnaise and lemon juice and pulse until a smooth consistency is achieved.

6. Take care when removing the chops from the fryer, then plate up and serve with the avocado mayo.

# SEAFOOD

# Crab Legs

**THE 4 SERVINGS CONTAIN: 150 CAL, 5.5 G FAT, 16.7 G PROTEIN, 0 G NET CARBS.**

## Ingredients

- ✓ 3 lb. crab legs
- ✓ ¼ cup salted butter, melted and divided
- ✓ ½ lemon, juiced
- ✓ ¼ tsp. garlic powder

## Method

1. In a bowl, toss the crab legs and two tablespoons of the melted butter together. Place the crab legs in the basket of the fryer.

2. Cook at 400°F for fifteen minutes, giving the basket a good shake halfway through.

3. Combine the remaining butter with the lemon juice and garlic powder.

4. Crack open the cooked crab legs and remove the meat. Serve with the butter dip on the side, and enjoy!

# Fish Sticks

**THE 4 SERVINGS CONTAIN: 273 CAL, 15 G FAT, 23.4 G PROTEIN, 0 G NET CARBS.**

## Ingredients

- ✓ 1 lb. whitefish
- ✓ 2 tbsp. Dijon mustard
- ✓ ¼ cup mayonnaise
- ✓ 1 ½ cup pork rinds, finely ground
- ✓ ¾ tsp. Cajun seasoning

## Method

1. Place the fish on a tissue to dry it off, then cut it up into slices about two inches thick.

2. In one bowl, combine the mustard and mayonnaise, and in another, the Cajun seasoning and pork rinds.

3. Coat the fish firstly in the mayo-mustard mixture, then in the Cajun-pork rind mixture. Give each slice a shake to remove any surplus. Then place the fish sticks in the basket of the air flyer.

4. Cook at 400°F for five minutes. Turn the fish sticks over and cook for another five minutes on the other side.

5. Serve warm with a dipping sauce of your choosing and enjoy.

# Crusty Pesto Salmon

**THE 2 SERVINGS CONTAIN: 423 CAL, 33 G FAT, 22.3 G PROTEIN, 1 G NET CARBS.**

## Ingredients

- ¼ cup almonds, roughly chopped
- ¼ cup pesto
- 2 x 4-oz. salmon fillets
- 2 tbsp. unsalted butter, melted

## Method

1. Mix the almonds and pesto together.

2. Place the salmon fillets in a round baking dish, roughly six inches in diameter.

3. Brush the fillets with butter, followed by the pesto mixture, ensuring to coat both the top and bottom. Put the baking dish inside the fryer.

4. Cook for twelve minutes at 390°F.

5. The salmon is ready when it flakes easily when prodded with a fork. Serve warm.

# Salmon Patties

**THE 2 SERVINGS CONTAIN: 318 CAL, 17 G FAT, 32.8 G PROTEIN, 0.5 G NET CARBS.**

## Ingredients

- 1 tsp. chili powder
- 2 tbsp. full-fat mayonnaise
- ¼ cup ground pork rinds
- 2 x 5-oz. pouches of cooked pink salmon
- 1 egg

## Method

1. Stir everything together to prepare the patty mixture. If the mixture is dry or falling apart, add in more pork rinds as necessary.

2. Take equal-sized amounts of the mixture to form four patties, before placing the patties in the basket of your air fryer.

3. Cook at 400°F for eight minutes.

4. Halfway through cooking, flip the patties over. Once they are crispy, serve with the toppings of your choice and enjoy.

# Cajun Salmon

**THE 2 SERVINGS CONTAIN: 255 CAL, 15.6 G FAT, 21.9 G PROTEIN, 0 G NET CARBS.**

## Ingredients

- ✓ 2 4-oz skinless salmon fillets
- ✓ 2 tbsp. unsalted butter, melted
- ✓ 1 pinch ground cayenne pepper
- ✓ 1 tsp. paprika
- ✓ ½ tsp. garlic pepper

## Method

1. Using a brush, apply the butter to the salmon fillets.

2. Combine the other ingredients and massage this mixture into the fillets. Lay the fish inside your fryer.

3. Cook for seven minutes at 390°F.

4. When the salmon is ready it should flake apart easily.

5. Enjoy with the sides of your choosing.

# Buttery Cod

**THE 2 SERVINGS CONTAIN: 175 CAL, 11.5 G FAT, 18.4 G PROTEIN, 0 G NET CARBS.**

## Ingredients

- ✓ 2 x 4-oz. cod fillets
- ✓ 2 tbsp. salted butter, melted
- ✓ 1 tsp. Old Bay seasoning
- ✓ ½ medium lemon, sliced

## Method

1. Place the cod fillets in a baking dish.

2. Brush with melted butter, season with Old Bay, and top with some lemon slices.

3. Wrap the fish in aluminum foil and put into your fryer.

4. Cook for eight minutes at 350°F.

5. The cod is ready when it flakes easily. Serve hot.

# Sesame Tuna Steak

**THE 4 SERVINGS CONTAIN: 118 CAL, 4.2 G FAT, 16.1 G PROTEIN, 0 G NET CARBS.**

## Ingredients

- ✓ 1 tbsp. coconut oil, melted
- ✓ 2 x 6-oz. tuna steaks
- ✓ ½ tsp. garlic powder
- ✓ 2 tsp. black sesame seeds
- ✓ 2 tsp. white sesame seeds

## Method

1. Apply the coconut oil to the tuna steaks with a brunch, then season with garlic powder.

2. Combine the black and white sesame seeds. Embed them in the tuna steaks, covering the fish all over. Place the tuna into your air fryer.

3. Cook for eight minutes at 400°F, turning the fish halfway through.

4. The tuna steaks are ready when they have reached a temperature of 145°F. Serve straightaway.

# Lemon Garlic Shrimp

**THE 4 SERVINGS CONTAIN: 195 CAL, 12.8 G FAT, 14.4 G PROTEIN, 1 G NET CARBS.**

## Ingredients

- ✓ 1 medium lemon
- ✓ ½ lb. medium shrimp, shelled and deveined
- ✓ ½ tsp. Old Bay seasoning
- ✓ 2 tbsp. unsalted butter, melted
- ✓ ½ tsp. minced garlic

## Method

1. Grate the rind of the lemon into a bowl. Cut the lemon in half and juice it over the same bowl. Toss in the shrimp, Old Bay, and butter, mixing everything to make sure the shrimp is completely covered.

2. Transfer to a round baking dish roughly six inches wide, then place this dish in your fryer.

3. Cook at 400°F for six minutes. The shrimp is cooked when it turns a bright pink color.

4. Serve hot, drizzling any leftover sauce over the shrimp.

# Foil Packet Salmon

**THE 2 SERVINGS CONTAIN: 222 CAL, 17.5 G FAT, 2.5 G PROTEIN, 0 G NET CARBS.**

## Ingredients

- ✓ 2 x 4-oz. skinless salmon fillets
- ✓ 2 tbsp. unsalted butter, melted
- ✓ ½ tsp. garlic powder
- ✓ 1 medium lemon
- ✓ ½ tsp. dried dill

## Method

1. Take a sheet of aluminum foil and cut into two squares measuring roughly 5" x 5". Lay each of the salmon fillets at the center of each piece. Brush both fillets with a tablespoon of bullet and season with a quarter-teaspoon of garlic powder.

2. Halve the lemon and grate the skin of one half over the fish. Cut four half-slices of lemon, using two to top each fillet. Season each fillet with a quarter-teaspoon of dill.

3. Fold the tops and sides of the aluminum foil over the fish to create a kind of packet. Place each one in the fryer.

4. Cook for twelve minutes at 400°F.

5. The salmon is ready when it flakes easily. Serve hot.

# Foil Packet Lobster Tail

**THE 2 SERVINGS CONTAIN: 239 CAL, 12.9 G FAT, 27.3 G PROTEIN, 0 G NET CARBS.**

## Ingredients

- ✓ 2 x 6-oz. lobster tail halves
- ✓ 2 tbsp. salted butter, melted
- ✓ ½ medium lemon, juiced
- ✓ ½ tsp. Old Bay seasoning
- ✓ 1 tsp. dried parsley

## Method

1. Lay each lobster on a sheet of aluminum foil. Pour a light drizzle of melted butter and lemon juice over each one, and season with Old Bay.

2. Fold down the sides and ends of the foil to seal the lobster. Place each one in the fryer.

3. Cook at 375°F for twelve minutes.

4. Just before serving, top the lobster with dried parsley.

# Avocado Shrimp

**THE 8 SERVINGS CONTAIN: 258 CAL, 21.9 G FAT, 6.5 G PROTEIN, 10 G NET CARBS.**

## Ingredients

- ✓ ½ cup onion, chopped
- ✓ 2 lb. shrimp
- ✓ 1 tbsp. seasoned salt
- ✓ 1 avocado
- ✓ ½ cup pecans, chopped

## Method

1. Pre-heat the fryer at 400°F.

2. Put the chopped onion in the basket of the fryer and spritz with some cooking spray. Leave to cook for five minutes.

3. Add the shrimp and set the timer for a further five minutes. Sprinkle with some seasoned salt, then allow to cook for an additional five minutes.

4. During these last five minutes, halve your avocado and remove the pit. Cube each half, then scoop out the flesh.

5. Take care when removing the shrimp from the fryer. Place it on a dish and top with the avocado and the chopped pecans.

# Lemon Butter Scallops

**THE 4 SERVINGS CONTAIN: 311 CAL, 27.8 G FAT, 12.5 G PROTEIN, 3 G NET CARBS.**

## Ingredients

- ✓ 1 lemon
- ✓ 1 lb. scallops
- ✓ ½ cup butter
- ✓ ¼ cup parsley, chopped

## Method

1. Juice the lemon into a Ziploc bag.

2. Wash your scallops, dry them, and season to taste. Put them in the bag with the lemon juice. Refrigerate for an hour.

3. Remove the bag from the refrigerator and leave for about twenty minutes until it returns to room temperature. Transfer the scallops into a foil pan that is small enough to be placed inside the fryer.

4. Pre-heat the fryer at 400°F and put the rack inside.

5. Place the foil pan on the rack, and cook for five minutes.

6. In the meantime, melt the butter in a saucepan over a medium heat. Zest the lemon over the saucepan, then add in the chopped parsley. Mix well.

7. Take care when removing the pan from the fryer. Transfer the contents to a plate and drizzle with the lemon-butter mixture. Serve hot.

# Cheesy Lemon Halibut

**THE 6 SERVINGS CONTAIN: 356 CAL, 32.2 G FAT, 14 G PROTEIN, 1.5 G NET CARBS.**

## Ingredients

- ✓ 1 lb. halibut fillet
- ✓ ½ cup butter
- ✓ 2 ½ tbsp. mayonnaise
- ✓ 2 ½ tbsp. lemon juice
- ✓ ¾ cup parmesan cheese, grated

## Method

1. Pre-heat your fryer at 375°F.

2. Spritz the halibut fillets with cooking spray and season as desired.

3. Put the halibut in the fryer and cook for twelve minutes..

4. In the meantime, combine the butter, mayonnaise, and lemon juice in a bowl with a hand mixer. Ensure a creamy texture is achieved.

5. Stir in the grated parmesan.

6. When the halibut is ready, open the drawer and spread the butter over the fish with a butter knife. Allow to cook for a further two minutes, then serve hot.

# Spicy Mackerel

**THE 2 SERVINGS CONTAIN: 415 CAL, 36.1 G FAT, 22 G PROTEIN, 1 G NET CARBS.**

## Ingredients

- ✓ 2 mackerel fillets
- ✓ 2 tbsp. red chili flakes
- ✓ 2 tsp. garlic, minced
- ✓ 1 tsp. lemon juice

## Method

1. Season the mackerel fillets with the red pepper flakes, minced garlic, and a drizzle of lemon juice. Allow to sit for five minutes.

2. Preheat your fryer at 350°F.

3. Cook the mackerel for five minutes, before opening the drawer, flipping the fillets, and allowing to cook on the other side for another five minutes.

4. Plate the fillets, making sure to spoon any remaining juice over them before serving.

# Thyme Scallops

**THE 2 SERVINGS CONTAIN: 254 CAL, 23.2 G FAT, 6.5 G PROTEIN, 8.7 G NET CARBS.**

## Ingredients

- ✓ 1 lb. scallops
- ✓ Salt and pepper
- ✓ ½ tbsp. butter
- ✓ ½ cup thyme, chopped

## Method

1. Wash the scallops and dry them completely. Season with pepper and salt, then set aside while you prepare the pan.

2. Grease a foil pan in several spots with the butter and cover the bottom with the thyme. Place the scallops on top.

3. Pre-heat the fryer at 400°F and set the rack inside.

4. Place the foil pan on the rack and allow to cook for seven minutes.

5. Take care when removing the pan from the fryer and transfer the scallops to a serving dish. Spoon any remaining butter in the pan over the fish and enjoy.

# Crispy Calamari

**THE 8 SERVINGS CONTAIN: 439 CAL, 37.7 G FAT, 15.3 G PROTEIN, 8.1 G NET CARBS.**

## Ingredients

- ✓ 1 lb. fresh squid
- ✓ Salt and pepper
- ✓ 2 cups almond flour
- ✓ 1 cup water
- ✓ 2 cloves garlic, minced
- ✓ ½ cup mayonnaise

## Method

1. Remove the skin from the squid and discard any ink. Slice the squid into rings and season with some salt and pepper.

2. Put the almond flour and water in separate bowls. Dip the squid firstly in the flour, then into the water, then into the almond flour again, ensuring that it is entirely covered with flour.

3. Pre-heat the fryer at 400°F. Put the squid inside and cook for six minutes.

4. In the meantime, prepare the aioli by combining the garlic with the mayonnaise in a bowl.

5. Once the squid is ready, plate up and serve with the aioli.

# Coconut Shrimp

**THE 6 SERVINGS CONTAIN: 345 CAL, 26.1 G FAT, 18.5 G PROTEIN, 5 G NET CARBS.**

## Ingredients

- ✓ 1 lb. shrimp
- ✓ Salt and pepper
- ✓ 2 cups grated coconut
- ✓ 2 eggs
- ✓ 1 cup coconut flour

## Method

1. Wash and peel the shrimp. Remove the heads, and devein.

2. Season with salt and pepper to taste and set aside.

3. Prepare three bowls to dip the shrimp into. Put the grated coconut into one, the lightly-beaten eggs into another, and the coconut flour into a third. Then proceed to dip the shrimp in the bowls in that order, making sure to coat each one well.

4. Pre-heat the fryer at 400°F.

5. Set the shrimp in the fryer and leave to cook for ten minutes. Check the shrimp is bright pink in color before serving. Leave to cook for another two minutes if you would like them browner. Serve hot.

# VEGAN & VEGETARIAN

# Parmesan Artichokes

**THE 4 SERVINGS CONTAIN: 188 CAL, 12.5 G FAT, 7.5 G PROTEIN, 1 G NET CARBS.**

## Ingredients

- ✓ 2 medium artichokes, trimmed and quartered, with the centers removed
- ✓ 2 tbsp. coconut oil, melted
- ✓ 1 egg, beaten
- ✓ ½ cup parmesan cheese, grated
- ✓ ¼ cup blanched, finely ground almond flour

## Method

1. Place the artichokes in a bowl with the coconut oil and toss to coat, then dip the artichokes into a bowl of beaten egg.

2. In a separate bowl, mix together the parmesan cheese and the almond flour. Combine with the pieces of artichoke, making sure to coat each piece well. Transfer the artichoke to the fryer.

3. Cook at 400°F for ten minutes, shaking occasionally throughout the cooking time. Serve hot.

# Cheese Pizza & Broccoli Crust

**THE 4 SERVINGS CONTAIN: 137 CAL, 7.5 G FAT, 9.8 G PROTEIN, 1.2 G NET CARBS.**

## Ingredients

- ✓ 3 cups broccoli rice, steamed
- ✓ ½ cup parmesan cheese, grated
- ✓ 1 egg
- ✓ 3 tbsp. low-carb Alfredo sauce
- ✓ ½ cup parmesan cheese, grated

## Method

1. Drain the broccoli rice and combine with the parmesan cheese and egg in a bowl, mixing well.

2. Cut a piece of parchment paper roughly the size of the base of the fryer's basket. Spoon four equal-sized amounts of the broccoli mixture onto the paper and press each portion into the shape of a pizza crust. You may have to complete this part in two batches. Transfer the parchment to the fryer.

3. Cook at 370°F for five minutes. When the crust is firm, flip it over and cook for an additional two minutes.

4. Add the Alfredo sauce and mozzarella cheese on top of the crusts and cook for an additional seven minutes. The crusts are ready when the sauce and cheese have melted. Serve hot.

# Cauliflower Steak

**THE 4 SERVINGS CONTAIN: 125 CAL, 8.3 G FAT, 4.8 G PROTEIN, 1.5 G NET CARBS.**

## Ingredients

- ✓ 1 medium head cauliflower
- ✓ 2 tbsp. coconut oil, melted
- ✓ ¼ cup hot sauce

## Method

1. Wash the cauliflower head and slice it into steaks about a half-inch thick each.

2. In a bowl, stir together the coconut oil and hot sauce to combine. Apply to the cauliflower using a brush. Place the steaks in the basket of your fryer. You may need to do this in batches.

3. Cook the steaks at 400°F for seven minutes until the edges are brown. Serve with the toppings of your choice.

# Stuffed Eggplant

**THE 2 SERVINGS CONTAIN: 285 CAL, 18.8 G FAT, 9.5 G PROTEIN, 1 G NET CARBS.**

## Ingredients

- ✓ 1 large eggplant
- ✓ ¼ medium yellow onion, diced
- ✓ 2 tbsp. red bell pepper, diced
- ✓ 1 cup spinach
- ✓ ¼ cup artichoke hearts, chopped

## Method

1. Cut the eggplant lengthwise into slices and spoon out the flesh, leaving a shell about a half-inch thick. Chop it up and set aside.

2. Set a skillet over a medium heat and spritz with cooking spray. Cook the onions for about three to five minutes to soften. Then add the pepper, spinach, artichokes, and the flesh of eggplant. Fry for a further five minutes, then remove from the heat.

3. Scoop this mixture in equal parts into the eggplant shells and place each one in the fryer.

4. Cook for twenty minutes at 320°F until the eggplant shells are soft. Serve warm.

# Broccoli Salad

**THE 2 SERVINGS CONTAIN: 225 CAL, 17.3 G FAT, 6.5 G PROTEIN, 2.5 G NET CARBS.**

## Ingredients

- ✓ 3 cups fresh broccoli florets
- ✓ 2 tbsp. coconut oil, melted
- ✓ ¼ cup sliced almonds
- ✓ ½ medium lemon, juiced

## Method

1. Take a six-inch baking dish and fill with the broccoli florets. Pour the melted coconut oil over the broccoli and add in the sliced almonds. Toss together. Put the dish in the air fryer.

2. Cook at 380°F for seven minutes, stirring at the halfway point.

3. Place the broccoli in a bowl and drizzle the lemon juice over it.

# Eggplant Caprese

**THE 4 SERVINGS CONTAIN: 185 CAL, 12.8 G FAT, 9.5 G PROTEIN, 2.5 G NET CARBS.**

## Ingredients

- ✓ 1 medium eggplant, cut into ¼-inch slices
- ✓ 2 large tomatoes cut into ¼-inch slices
- ✓ 4 oz. fresh mozzarella cut into ½-oz slices
- ✓ 2 tbsp. olive oil
- ✓ A few sprigs of fresh basil

## Method

1. Cover the bottom of a baking dish with the eggplant slices. Place a tomato slice on top, followed by the mozzarella, and top with another piece of eggplant. Continue in this way until you have used all the ingredients.

2. Splash some olive oil on top and wrap some foil around the dish. Place it into your fryer.

3. Cook at 350°F for twelve minutes.

4. Check the eggplants have softened before serving. Top with some fresh basil.

# Roasted Cauliflower

**THE 4 SERVINGS CONTAIN: 95 CAL, 5.8 G FAT, 2 G PROTEIN, 1 G NET CARBS.**

## Ingredients

- ✓ 1 medium head cauliflower
- ✓ 2 tbsp. salted butter, melted
- ✓ 1 medium lemon
- ✓ 1 tsp. dried parsley
- ✓ ½ tsp. garlic powder

## Method

1. Having removed the leaves from the cauliflower head, brush it with the melted butter. Grate the rind of the lemon over it and then drizzle some juice. Finally add the parsley and garlic powder on top.

2. Transfer the cauliflower to the basket of the fryer.

3. Cook for fifteen minutes at 350°F, checking regularly to ensure it doesn't overcook. The cauliflower is ready when it is hot and fork tender.

4. Take care when removing it from the fryer, cut up and serve.

# Mushroom Loaf

**THE 8 SERVINGS CONTAIN: 355 CAL, 35.6 G FAT, 11.4 G PROTEIN, 4.5 G NET CARBS.**

## Ingredients

- ✓ 2 cups mushrooms, chopped
- ✓ ½ cups cheddar cheese, shredded
- ✓ ¾ cup almond flour
- ✓ 2 tbsp. butter, melted
- ✓ 2 eggs

## Method

1. In a food processor, pulse together the mushrooms, cheese, almond flour, melted butter, and eggs, along with some salt and pepper if desired, until a uniform consistency is achieved.

2. Transfer into a silicone loaf pan, spreading and levelling with a palette knife.

3. Pre-heat the fryer at 375°F and put the rack inside.

4. Set the loaf pan on the rack and cook for fifteen minutes.

5. Take care when removing the pan from the fryer and leave it to cool. Then slice and serve.

# Green Bean Casserole

**THE 8 SERVINGS CONTAIN: 359 CAL, 36.1 G FAT, 15.3 G PROTEIN, 1.5 G NET CARBS.**

## Ingredients

- ✓ 1 tbsp. butter, melted
- ✓ 1 cup green beans
- ✓ 6 oz. cheddar cheese, shredded
- ✓ 7 oz. parmesan cheese, shredded
- ✓ ¼ cup heavy cream

## Method

1. Pre-heat your fryer at 400°F.

2. Take a baking dish small enough to fit inside the fryer and cover the bottom with melted butter. Throw in the green beans, cheddar cheese, and any seasoning as desired, then give it a stir. Add the parmesan on top and finally the heavy cream.

3. Cook in the fryer for six minutes. Allow to cool before serving.

# Cabbage Steaks

**THE 4 SERVINGS CONTAIN: 36 CAL, 2.5 G FAT, 1.9 G PROTEIN, 2.5 G NET CARBS.**

## Ingredients

- ✓ 1 small head cabbage
- ✓ 1 tsp. butter, butter
- ✓ 1 tsp. paprika
- ✓ 1 tsp. olive oil

## Method

1. Halve the cabbage.

2. In a bowl, mix together the melted butter, paprika, and olive oil. Massage into the cabbage slices, making sure to coat it well. Season as desired with salt and pepper or any other seasonings of your choosing.

3. Pre-heat the fryer at 400°F and set the rack inside.

4. Put the cabbage in the fryer and cook for three minutes. Flip it and cook on the other side for another two minutes. Enjoy!

# Zucchini Gratin

**THE 6 SERVINGS CONTAIN: 97 CAL, 5 G FAT, 7.5 G PROTEIN, 2.8 G NET CARBS.**

## Ingredients

- ✓ oz. parmesan cheese, shredded
- ✓ 1 tbsp. coconut flour
- ✓ 1 tbsp. dried parsley
- ✓ 2 zucchini
- ✓ 1 tsp. butter, melted

## Method

1. Mix the parmesan and coconut flour together in a bowl, seasoning with parsley to taste.

2. Cut the zucchini in half lengthwise and chop the halves into four slices.

3. Pre-heat the fryer at 400°F.

4. Pour the melted butter over the zucchini and then dip the zucchini into the parmesan-flour mixture, coating it all over. Cook the zucchini in the fryer for thirteen minutes.

# Cheesy Kale

**THE 7 SERVINGS CONTAIN: 181 CAL, 12.2 G FAT, 11.9 G PROTEIN, 5 G NET CARBS.**

## Ingredients

- ✓ 1 lb. kale
- ✓ 8 oz. parmesan cheese, shredded
- ✓ 1 onion, diced
- ✓ 1 tsp. butter
- ✓ 1 cup heavy cream

## Method

1. Dice up the kale, discarding any hard stems. In a baking dish small enough to fit inside the fryer, combine the kale with the parmesan, onion, butter and cream.

2. Pre-heat the fryer at 250°F.

3. Set the baking dish in the fryer and cook for twelve minutes. Make sure to give it a good stir before serving.

# Spaghetti Squash

**THE 8 SERVINGS CONTAIN: 53 CAL, 3.2 G FAT, 1.7 G PROTEIN, 5.7 G NET CARBS.**

## Ingredients

- ✓ 1 spaghetti squash
- ✓ 1 tsp. olive oil
- ✓ Salt and pepper
- ✓ tbsp. heavy cream
- ✓ 1 tsp. butter

## Method

1. Pre-heat your fryer at 360°F.

2. Cut and de-seed the spaghetti squash. Brush with the olive oil and season with salt and pepper to taste.

3. Put the squash inside the fryer, placing it cut-side-down. Cook for thirty minutes. Halfway through cooking, fluff the spaghetti inside the squash with a fork.

4. When the squash is ready, fluff the spaghetti some more, then pour some heavy cream and butter over it and give it a good stir. Serve with the low-carb tomato sauce of your choice.

# SNACKS &
# SIDE DISHES

# Mini Pepper Poppers

**THE 16 SERVINGS CONTAIN: 177 CAL, 12.4 G FAT, 7.5 G PROTEIN, 1.7 G NET CARBS.**

## Ingredients

- ✓ 8 mini sweet peppers
- ✓ ¼ cup pepper jack cheese, shredded
- ✓ 4 slices sugar-free bacon, cooked and crumbled
- ✓ 4 oz. full-fat cream cheese, softened

## Method

1. Prepare the peppers by cutting off the tops and halving them lengthwise. Then take out the membrane and the seeds.

2. In a small bowl, combine the pepper jack cheese, bacon, and cream cheese, making sure to incorporate everything well.

3. Spoon equal-sized portions of the cheese-bacon mixture into each of the pepper halves.

4. Place the peppers inside your fryer and cook for eight minutes at 400°F. Take care when removing them from the fryer, and enjoy warm.

# Bacon-Wrapped Jalapeno Popper

**THE 4 SERVINGS CONTAIN: 226 CAL, 18.9 G FAT, 12.4 G PROTEIN, 1.5 G NET CARBS.**

## Ingredients

- ✓ Jalapenos
- ✓ 1/3 cup medium cheddar cheese, shredded
- ✓ ¼ tsp. garlic powder
- ✓ 3 oz. full-fat cream cheese
- ✓ 12 slices sugar-free bacon

## Method

1. Prepare the jalapenos by slicing off the tops and halving each one lengthwise. Take care when removing the seeds and membranes, wearing gloves if necessary.

2. In a microwavable bowl, combine the cheddar cheese, garlic powder, and cream cheese. Microwave for half a minute and mix again, before spoon equal parts of this mixture into each of the jalapeno halves.

3. Take a slice of bacon and wrap it around one of the jalapeno halves, covering it entirely. Place it in the basket of your fryer. Repeat with the rest of the bacon and jalapenos.

4. Cook at 400°F for twelve minutes, flipping the peppers halfway through in order to ensure the bacon gets crispy. Make sure not to let any of the contents spill out of the jalapeno halves when turning them.

5. Eat the peppers hot or at room temperature.

# Cheesy Jalapeno Bacon Bread

**THE 8 SERVINGS CONTAIN: 263 CAL, 17.1 G FAT, 20.5 G PROTEIN, 1 G NET CARBS.**

## Ingredients

- ✓ slices sugar-free bacon, cooked and chopped
- ✓ 2 eggs
- ✓ ¼ cup pickled jalapenos, chopped
- ✓ ¼ cup parmesan cheese, grated
- ✓ 2 cups mozzarella cheese, shredded

## Method

1. Add all of the ingredients together in a bowl and mix together.

2. Cut out a piece of parchment paper that will fit the base of your fryer's basket. Place it inside the fryer.

3. With slightly wet hands, roll the mixture into a circle. You may have to form two circles to cook in separate batches, depending on the size of your fryer.

4. Place the circle on top of the parchment paper inside your fryer. Cook at 320°F for ten minutes.

5. Turn the bread over and cook for another five minutes.

6. The bread is ready when it is golden and cooked all the way through. Slice and serve warm.

# Low-Carb Pizza Crust

**THE 1 SERVING CONTAINS: 330 CAL, 21.7 G FAT, 18.9 G PROTEIN, 2.5 G NET CARBS.**

## Ingredients

- ✓ 1 tbsp. full-fat cream cheese
- ✓ ½ cup whole-milk mozzarella cheese, shredded
- ✓ 2 tbsp. blanched finely ground almond flour
- ✓ 1 egg white

## Method

1. In a microwave-safe bowl, combine the cream cheese, mozzarella, and almond flour and heat in the microwave for half a minute. Mix well to create a smooth consistency. Add in the egg white and stir to form a soft ball of dough.

2. With slightly wet hands, press the dough into a pizza crust about six inches in diameter.

3. Place a sheet of parchment paper in the bottom of your fryer and lay the crust on top. Cook for ten minutes at 350°F, turning the crust over halfway through the cooking time.

4. Top the pizza base with the toppings of your choice and enjoy!

# Bacon-Wrapped Onion Rings

**THE 4 SERVINGS CONTAIN: 115 CAL, 5.7 G FAT, 7.6 G PROTEIN, 3.4 G NET CARBS.**

## Ingredients

- ✓ 1 large onion, peeled
- ✓ 8 slices sugar-free bacon
- ✓ 1 tbsp. sriracha

## Method

1. Chop up the onion into slices a quarter-inch thick. Gently pull apart the rings. Take a slice of bacon and wrap it around an onion ring. Repeat with the rest of the ingredients. Place each onion ring in your fryer.

2. Cut the onion rings at 350°F for ten minutes, turning them halfway through to ensure the bacon crisps up.

3. Serve hot with the sriracha.

# Mozzarella Sticks

**THE 12 SERVINGS CONTAIN: 216 CAL, 11.8 G FAT, 17.2 G PROTEIN, 4.4 G NET CARBS.**

## Ingredients

- ✓ x 1-oz. mozzarella string cheese sticks
- ✓ 1 tsp. dried parsley
- ✓ ½ oz. pork rinds, finely ground
- ✓ ½ cup parmesan cheese, grated
- ✓ 2 eggs

## Method

1. Halve the mozzarella sticks and freeze for forty-five minutes. Optionally you can leave them longer and place in a Ziploc bag to prevent them from becoming freezer-burned.

2. In a small bowl, combine the dried parsley, pork rinds, and parmesan cheese.

3. In a separate bowl, beat the eggs with a fork.

4. Take a frozen mozzarella stick and dip it into the eggs, then into the pork rind mixture, making sure to coat it all over. Proceed with the rest of the cheese sticks, placing each coated stick in the basket of your air fryer.

5. Cook at 400°F for ten minutes, until they are golden brown.

6. Serve hot, with some homemade marinara sauce if desired.

# Beef Jerky

**THE 10 SERVINGS CONTAIN: 87 CAL, 3.7 G FAT, 10.5 G PROTEIN, 0.8 G NET CARBS.**

## Ingredients

- ✓ ¼ tsp. garlic powder
- ✓ ¼ tsp. onion powder
- ✓ ¼ cup soy sauce
- ✓ 2 tsp. Worcestershire sauce
- ✓ 1 lb. flat iron steak, thinly sliced

## Method

1. In a bowl, combine the garlic powder, onion powder, soy sauce, and Worcestershire sauce. Marinade the beef slices with the mixture in an airtight bag, shaking it well to ensure the beef is well-coated. Leave to marinate for at least two hours.

2. Place the meat in the basket of your air fryer, making sure it is evenly-spaced. Cook the beef slices in more than one batch if necessary.

3. Cook for four hours at 160°F.

4. Allow to cool before serving. You can keep the jerky in an airtight container for up to a week, if you can resist it that long.

# Smoked BBQ Toasted Almonds

**THE 4 SERVINGS CONTAIN: 172 CAL, 15.3 G FAT, 6.1 G PROTEIN, 0 G NET CARBS.**

## Ingredients

- ✓ 2 tsp. coconut oil, melted
- ✓ ¼ tsp. smoked paprika
- ✓ 1 tsp. chili powder
- ✓ ¼ tsp. cumin
- ✓ 1 cup raw almonds

## Method

1. Mix the melted coconut oil with the paprika, chili powder, and cumin. Place the almonds in a large bowl and pour the coconut oil over them, tossing them to cover them evenly.

2. Place the almonds in the basket of your fryer and spread them out across the base.

3. Cook for six minutes at 320°F, giving the basket an occasional shake to make sure everything is cooked evenly.

4. Leave to cool and serve.

# Bacon-Wrapped Brie

**THE 8 SERVINGS CONTAIN: 126 CAL, 8.8 G FAT, 7.5 G PROTEIN, 0 G NET CARBS.**

## Ingredients

- ✓ slices sugar-free bacon
- ✓ 8 oz. brie cheese

## Method

1. On a cutting board, lay out the slices of bacon across each other in a star shape (two Xs overlaid). Then place the entire round of brie in the center of this star.

2. Lift each slice of bacon to wrap it over the brie and use toothpicks to hold everything in place. Cut up a piece of parchment paper to fit in your fryer's basket and place it inside, followed by the wrapped brie, setting it in the center of the sheet of parchment.

3. Cook at 400°F for seven minutes. Turn the brie over and cook for a further three minutes.

4. It is ready once the bacon is crispy and cheese is melted on the inside.

5. Slice up the brie and enjoy hot.

# Crust-less Meaty Pizza

**THE 1 SERVING CONTAINS: 446 CAL, 35 G FAT, 27.1 G PROTEIN, 4.5 G NET CARBS.**

## Ingredients

- ✓ ½ cup mozzarella cheese, shredded
- ✓ 2 slices sugar-free bacon, cooked and crumbled
- ✓ ¼ cup ground sausage, cooked
- ✓ 7 slices pepperoni
- ✓ 1 tbsp. parmesan cheese, grated

## Method

1. Spread the mozzarella across the bottom of a six-inch cake pan. Throw on the bacon, sausage, and pepperoni, then add a sprinkle of the parmesan cheese on top. Place the pan inside your air fryer.

2. Cook at 400°F for five minutes. The cheese is ready once brown in color and bubbly. Take care when removing the pan from the fryer and serve.

# Cheesy Garlic Bread

**THE 2 SERVINGS CONTAIN: 278 CAL, 15.6 G FAT, 17.2 G PROTEIN, 3.3 G NET CARBS.**

## Ingredients

- ✓ ½ tsp. garlic powder
- ✓ 1 egg
- ✓ ¼ cup parmesan cheese, grated
- ✓ 1 cup mozzarella cheese, shredded

## Method

1. Mix all the ingredients together in a large bowl. Cut a piece of parchment to fit the bottom of your fryer's basket. Pour the mixture onto the paper to form a circle. Transfer this to the air fryer.

2. Cook for ten minutes at 350°F.

3. Slice up the bread and enjoy.

# Avocado Fries

**THE 4 SERVINGS CONTAIN: 256 CAL, 21.1 G FAT, 6.7 G PROTEIN, 1.2 G NET CARBS.**

## Ingredients

- ✓ 2 medium avocados
- ✓ 1 oz. pork rind, finely ground

## Method

1. Halve the avocados and remove their pits. Scoop out the flesh and slice it up about a quarter-inch thick.

2. In a bowl, coat the avocado with the pork rinds, then transfer the avocado slices to the basket of the fryer.

3. Cook at 350°F for five minutes and serve right away.

# Roasted Eggplant

**THE 4 SERVINGS CONTAIN: 98 CAL, 6.5 G FAT, 1.2 G PROTEIN, 2.5 G NET CARBS.**

## Ingredients

- ✓ 1 large eggplant
- ✓ 2 tbsp. olive oil
- ✓ ¼ tsp. salt
- ✓ ½ tsp. garlic powder

## Method

1. Prepare the eggplant by slicing off the top and bottom and cutting it into slices around a quarter-inch thick.

2. Apply olive oil to the slices with a brush, coating both sides. Season each side with sprinklings of salt and garlic powder.

3. Place the slices in the fryer and cook for fifteen minutes at 390°F.

4. Serve straight away.

---

# Low-Carb Pita Chips

**THE 4 SERVINGS CONTAIN: 165 CAL, 15.6 G FAT, 12.3 G PROTEIN, 1 G NET CARBS.**

## Ingredients

- ✓ 1 cup mozzarella cheese, shredded
- ✓ 1 egg
- ✓ ¼ cup blanched finely ground almond flour
- ✓ ½ oz. pork rinds, finely ground

## Method

1. Melt the mozzarella in the microwave. Add the egg, almond flour, and pork rinds and combine together to form a smooth paste. Microwave the cheese again if it begins to set.

2. Put the dough between two sheets of parchment paper and use a rolling pin to flatten it out into a rectangle. The thickness is up to you. With a sharp knife, cut into the dough to form triangles. It may be necessary to complete this step in multiple batches.

3. Place the chips in the fryer and cook for five minutes at 350°F. Turn them over and cook on the other side for another five minutes, or until the chips are golden and firm.

4. Allow the chips to cool and harden further. They can be stored in an airtight container.

# Fried Pickles

**THE 4 SERVINGS CONTAIN: 87 CAL, 6.2 G FAT, 4.1 G PROTEIN, 1 G NET CARBS.**

## Ingredients

- ¼ tsp. garlic powder
- 1 tbsp. coconut flour
- 1/3 cup blanched finely ground almond flour
- 1 egg
- 1 cup sliced pickles

## Method

1. In a bowl, stir together the garlic powder, coconut flour, and almond flour to combine well. In a separate bowl, beat the egg with a fork.

2. Make sure the pickle slices are dry. Dredge them in the egg, then dip them into the flour mixture, making sure to coat them well. Place the pickles in your fryer, careful not overlap them. If necessary, cook them in multiple batches.

3. Cook the pickles at 400°F for five minutes. Turn them over and cook for a further three minutes.

4. Enjoy the pickles with the dipping sauce of your choosing.

# Kale Chips

**THE 4 SERVINGS CONTAIN: 25 CAL, 2.1 G FAT, 0.6 G PROTEIN, 0 G NET CARBS.**

## Ingredients

- cups stemmed kale
- ½ tsp. salt
- 2 tsp. avocado oil

## Method

1. In a large bowl, toss together the kale, salt, and avocado oil, softening the kale with your hands. Transfer everything into the basket of your fryer.

2. Cook at 400°F for five minutes, shaking occasionally throughout the cooking time to ensure the chips are crispy and evenly cooked.

3. Serve with your favorite dips.

# Flatbread

**THE 2 SERVINGS CONTAIN: 276 CAL, 21.6 G FAT, 15.3 G PROTEIN, 1.7 G NET CARBS.**

## Ingredients

- ✓ 1 cup mozzarella cheese, shredded
- ✓ ¼ cup blanched finely ground almond flour
- ✓ 1 oz. full-fat cream cheese, softened

## Method

1. Microwave the mozzarella for half a minute until melted. Combine with the almond flour to achieve a smooth consistency, before adding the cream cheese. Keep mixing to create a dough, microwaving the mixture again if the cheese begins to harden.

2. Divide the dough into two equal pieces. Between two sheets of parchment paper, roll out the dough until it is about a quarter-inch thick. Cover the bottom of your fryer with another sheet of parchment.

3. Transfer the dough into the fryer and cook at 320°F for seven minutes. You may need to complete this step in two batches. Make sure to turn the flatbread halfway through cooking. Take care when removing it from the fryer and serve warm.

# Radish Chips

**THE 4 SERVINGS CONTAIN: 75 CAL, 6.4 G FAT, 0.4 G PROTEIN, 1 G NET CARBS.**

## Ingredients

- ✓ 2 cups water
- ✓ 1 lb. radishes
- ✓ ½ tsp. garlic powder
- ✓ ¼ tsp. onion powder
- ✓ 2 tbsp. coconut oil, melted

## Method

1. Boil the water over the stove.

2. In the meantime, prepare the radish chips. Slice off the tops and bottoms and, using a mandolin, shave into thin slices of equal size. Alternatively this step can be completed using your food processor if it has a slicing blade.

3. Put the radish chips in the pot of boiling water and allow to cook for five minutes, ensuring they become translucent. Take care when removing from the water and place them on a paper towel to dry.

4. Add the radish chips, garlic powder, onion powder, and melted coconut oil into a bowl and toss to coat. Transfer the chips to your fryer.

5. Cook at 320°F for five minutes, occasionally giving the basket a good shake to ensure even cooking. The chips are done when cooked through and crispy. Serve immediately.

# Parmesan Zucchini Chips

**THE 4 SERVINGS CONTAIN: 120 CAL, 6.5 G FAT, 9.5 G PROTEIN, 2 G NET CARBS.**

## Ingredients

- ✓ 2 medium zucchini
- ✓ 1 oz. pork rinds, finely ground
- ✓ ½ cup parmesan cheese, grated
- ✓ 1 egg

## Method

1. Cut the zucchini into slices about a quarter-inch thick. Lay on a paper towel to dry.

2. In a bowl, combine the ground pork rinds and the grated parmesan.

3. In a separate bowl, beat the egg with a fork.

4. Take a zucchini slice and dip it into the egg, then into the pork rind-parmesan mixture, making sure to coat it evenly. Repeat with the rest of the slices. Lay them in the basket of your fryer, taking care not to overlap. This step may need to be completed in more than one batch.

5. Cook at 320°F for five minutes. Turn the chips over and allow to cook for another five minutes.

6. Allow to cool to achieve a crispier texture, or serve warm. Enjoy!

# Buffalo Cauliflower

**THE 4 SERVINGS CONTAIN: 85 CAL, 5.5 G FAT, 2 G PROTEIN, 3 G NET CARBS.**

## Ingredients

- ✓ ½ packet dry ranch seasoning
- ✓ 2 tbsp. salted butter, melted
- ✓ Cauliflower florets
- ✓ ¼ cup buffalo sauce

## Method

1. In a bowl, combine the dry ranch seasoning and butter. Toss with the cauliflower florets to coat and transfer them to the fryer.

2. Cook at 400°F for five minutes, shaking the basket occasionally to ensure the florets cook evenly.

3. Remove the cauliflower from the fryer, pour the buffalo sauce over it, and enjoy.

# Zesty Cilantro Roasted Cauliflower

**THE 4 SERVINGS CONTAIN: 76 CAL, 6.2 G FAT, 1 G PROTEIN, 1.5 G NET CARBS.**

## Ingredients

- ✓ 2 cups cauliflower florets, chopped
- ✓ 2 tbsp. coconut oil, melted
- ✓ 2 ½ tsp. taco seasoning mix
- ✓ 1 medium lime
- ✓ 2 tbsp. cilantro, chopped

## Method

1. Mix the cauliflower with the melted coconut oil and the taco seasoning, ensuring to coat the florets all over.

2. Cook at 350°F for seven minutes, shaking the basket a few times through the cooking time. Then transfer the cauliflower to a bowl.

3. Squeeze the lime juice over the cauliflower and season with the cilantro. Toss once more to coat and enjoy.

# Brussels Sprout Chips

**THE 4 SERVINGS CONTAIN: 99 CAL, 6 G FAT, 2 G PROTEIN, 1 G NET CARBS.**

## Ingredients

- ✓ 1 lb. Brussels sprouts
- ✓ 1 tbsp. coconut oil, melted
- ✓ 1 tbsp. unsalted butter, melted

## Method

1. Prepare the Brussels sprouts by halving them, discarding any loose leaves.

2. Combine with the melted coconut oil and transfer to your air fryer.

3. Cook at 400°F for ten minutes, giving the basket a good shake throughout the cooking time to brown them up if desired.

4. The sprouts are ready when they are partially caramelized. Remove them from the fryer and serve with a topping of melted butter before serving.

# Cauliflower Tots

**THE 4 SERVINGS CONTAIN: 171 CAL, 9.5 G FAT, 12.5 G PROTEIN, 3 G NET CARBS.**

## Ingredients

- ✓ 1 large head cauliflower
- ✓ ½ cup parmesan cheese, grated
- ✓ 1 cup mozzarella cheese, shredded
- ✓ 1 tsp. seasoned salt
- ✓ 1 egg

## Method

1. Place a steamer basket over a pot of boiling water, ensuring the water is not high enough to enter the basket.
2. Cut up the cauliflower into florets and transfer to the steamer basket. Cover the pot with a lid and leave to steam for seven minutes, making sure the cauliflower softens.
3. Place the florets on a cheesecloth and leave to cool. Remove as much moisture as possible. This is crucial as it ensures the cauliflower will harden.
4. In a bowl, break up the cauliflower with a fork.
5. Stir in the parmesan, mozzarella, seasoned salt, and egg, incorporating the cauliflower well with all of the other ingredients. Make sure the mixture is firm enough to be moldable.
6. Using your hand, mold about two tablespoons of the mixture into tots and repeat until you have used up all of the mixture. Put each tot into your air fryer basket. They may need to be cooked in multiple batches.
7. Cook at 320°F for twelve minutes, turning them halfway through. Ensure they are brown in color before serving.

# Fried Green Tomatoes

**THE 4 SERVINGS CONTAIN: 116 CAL, 6.5 G FAT, 6.7 G PROTEIN, 3 G NET CARBS.**

## Ingredients

- ✓ 2 medium green tomatoes
- ✓ 1 egg
- ✓ ¼ cup blanched finely ground almond flour
- ✓ 1/3 cup parmesan cheese, grated

## Method

1. Slice the tomatoes about a half-inch thick.

2. Crack the egg into a bowl and beat it with a whisk. In a separate bowl, mix together the almond flour and parmesan cheese.

3. Dredge the tomato slices in egg, then dip them into the flour-cheese mixture to coat. Place each slice into the fryer basket. They may need to be cooked in multiple batches.

4. Cook at 400°F for seven minutes, turning them halfway through the cooking time, and then serve warm.

# Herbed Garlic Radishes

**THE 4 SERVINGS CONTAIN: 66 CAL, 5.5 G FAT, 0.6 G PROTEIN, 1.1 G NET CARBS.**

## Ingredients

- ✓ 1 lb. radishes
- ✓ 2 tbsp. unsalted butter, melted
- ✓ ¼ tsp. dried oregano
- ✓ ½ tsp. dried parsley
- ✓ ½ tsp. garlic powder

## Method

1. Prepare the radishes by cutting off their tops and bottoms and quartering them.

2. In a bowl, combine the butter, dried oregano, dried parsley, and garlic powder. Toss with the radishes to coat.

3. Transfer the radishes to your air fryer and cook at 350°F for ten minutes, shaking the basket at the halfway point to ensure the radishes cook evenly through. The radishes are ready when they begin to turn brown.

# Jicama Fries

**THE 4 SERVINGS CONTAIN: 95 CAL, 6.5 G FAT, 2.8 G PROTEIN, 1.5 G NET CARBS.**

## Ingredients

- ✓ 1 small jicama, peeled
- ✓ ¼ tsp. onion powder
- ✓ ¾ tsp. chili powder
- ✓ ¼ tsp. garlic powder
- ✓ ¼ tsp. ground black pepper

## Method

1. To make the fries, cut the jicama into matchsticks of your desired thickness.

2. In a bowl, toss them with the onion powder, chili powder, garlic powder, and black pepper to coat. Transfer the fries into the basket of your air fryer.

3. Cook at 350°F for twenty minutes, giving the basket an occasional shake throughout the cooking process. The fries are ready when they are hot and golden in color. Enjoy!

# Zesty Salmon Jerky

**THE 4 SERVINGS CONTAIN: 118 CAL, 4.5 G FAT, 14.1 G PROTEIN, 0 G NET CARBS.**

## Ingredients

- ✓ 1 lb. boneless skinless salmon
- ✓ ½ tsp. liquid smoke
- ✓ ½ tsp. ground ginger
- ✓ ¼ cup soy sauce
- ✓ ¼ tsp. red pepper flakes

## Method

1. Cut the salmon into strips about four inches long and a quarter-inch thick.

2. Put the salmon in an airtight container or bag along with the liquid smoke, ginger, soy sauce, and red pepper flakes, combining everything to coat the salmon completely. Leave the salmon in the refrigerator for at least two hours.

3. Transfer the salmon slices in the fryer, taking care not to overlap any pieces. This step may need to be completed in multiple batches.

4. Cook at 140°F for four hours.

5. Take care when removing the salmon from the fryer and leave it to cool. This jerky makes a good snack and can be stored in an airtight container.

# Avocado Sticks

**THE 6 SERVINGS CONTAIN: 320 CAL, 32.8 G FAT, 4.7 G PROTEIN, 8.7 G NET CARBS.**

## Ingredients

- ✓ 2 avocados
- ✓ 4 egg yolks
- ✓ 1 ½ tbsp. water
- ✓ Salt and pepper
- ✓ 1 cup almond flour
- ✓ 1 cup herbed butter

## Method

1. Halve the avocados, twist to open, and take out the pits. Cut each half into three equal slices.

2. In a bowl, combine the egg yolks and water. Season with salt and pepper to taste and whisk together.

3. Pour the almond flour into a shallow bowl.

4. Coat each slice of avocado in the almond flour, then in the egg, before dipping it in the almond flour again. Ensure the flour coats the avocado well and firmly.

5. Pre-heat the fryer at 400°F. When it is warm, put the avocados inside and cook for eight minutes.

6. Take care when removing the avocados from the fryer and enjoy with a side of the herbed butter.

# Zucchini Bites

**THE 4 SERVINGS CONTAIN: 215 CAL, 18.9 G FAT, 9.5 G PROTEIN, 11.6 G NET CARBS.**

## Ingredients

- ✓ Zucchini
- ✓ 1 egg
- ✓ ½ cup parmesan cheese, grated
- ✓ 1 tbsp. Italian herbs
- ✓ 1 cup coconut, grated

## Method

1. Thinly grate the zucchini and dry with a cheesecloth, ensuring to remove all of the moisture.

2. In a bowl, combine the zucchini with the egg, parmesan, Italian herbs, and grated coconut, mixing well to incorporate everything. Using your hands, mold the mixture into balls.

3. Pre-heat the fryer at 400°F and place a rack inside. Lay the zucchini balls on the rack and cook for ten minutes. Serve hot.

# Cheesy Cauliflower Bites

**THE 4 SERVINGS CONTAIN: 165 CAL, 12 G FAT, 6.5 G PROTEIN, 5.5 G NET CARBS.**

## Ingredients

- ✓ 2 cup cauliflower florets
- ✓ ¾ cup cheddar cheese, shredded
- ✓ ½ cup onion, chopped
- ✓ 1 tsp. seasoning salt
- ✓ 2 tbsp. butter, melted
- ✓ 2 cloves garlic, minced

## Method

1. Pulse the cauliflower florets in the food processor until they become crumbly. Use a cheesecloth to remove all the moisture from the cauliflower.

2. In a bowl, combine the cauliflower with the cheese, onion, seasoning salt, and melted butter. With your hands, roll the mixture into balls.

3. Pre-heat the fryer at 400°F.

4. Fry the balls for fourteen minutes, leaving them in the fryer for an additional two minutes if you like them browner. Serve hot.

# Pop Corn Broccoli

**THE 4 SERVINGS CONTAIN: 212 CAL, 18.5 G FAT, 4.1 G PROTEIN, 7.5 G NET CARBS.**

## Ingredients

- ✓ egg yolks
- ✓ ¼ cup butter, melted
- ✓ 2 cups coconut flower
- ✓ Salt and pepper
- ✓ 2 cups broccoli florets

## Method

1. In a bowl, whisk the egg yolks and melted butter together. Throw in the coconut flour, salt and pepper, then stir again to combine well.

2. Pre-heat the fryer at 400°F.

3. Dip each broccoli floret into the mixture and place in the fryer. Cook for six minutes, in multiple batches if necessary. Take care when removing them from the fryer and enjoy!

# Rosemary Green Beans

**THE 2 SERVINGS CONTAIN: 71 CAL, 6.2 G FAT, .7 G PROTEIN, 4 G NET CARBS.**

## Ingredients

- ✓ 1 tbsp. butter, melted
- ✓ 2 tbsp. rosemary
- ✓ ½ tsp. salt
- ✓ 3 cloves garlic, minced
- ✓ ¾ cup green beans, chopped

## Method

1. Pre-heat your fryer at 390°F.

2. Combine the melted butter with the rosemary, salt, and minced garlic. Toss in the green beans, making sure to coat them well.

3. Cook in the fryer for five minutes.

# Brussels Sprouts & Cheese Sauce

**THE 2 SERVINGS CONTAIN: 214 CAL, 17.1 G FAT, 11.1 G PROTEIN, 4.5 G NET CARBS.**

## Ingredients

- ✓ ¾ cups Brussels sprouts
- ✓ 1 tbsp. extra virgin olive oil
- ✓ ¼ tsp. salt
- ✓ ¼ cup mozzarella cheese, shredded

## Method

1. Halve the Brussels sprouts and drizzle with the olive oil. Season with salt and toss to coat.

2. Pre-heat your fryer at 375°F. When warm, transfer the Brussels sprouts inside and add the shredded mozzarella on top.

3. Cook for five minutes, serving when the cheese is melted.

# DESSERTS

# Peanut Butter Cookies

**THE 8 SERVINGS CONTAIN: 235 CAL, 18.5 G FAT, 7.7 G PROTEIN, 1 G NET CARBS.**

## Ingredients

- ✓ 1 cup no-sugar-added smooth peanut butter
- ✓ 1 egg
- ✓ 1 tsp. vanilla extract
- ✓ 1/3 cup granular erythritol

## Method

1. In a large bowl, combine all the ingredients until a smooth consistency is achieved and the mixture has begun to thicken.

2. Take eight equal-sized amounts of the mixture and mold each one into a ball. Flatten them with your palm to form cookies about two inches thick.

3. Cover the bottom of your fryer with a sheet of parchment paper and lay the cookies inside. This step may need to be completed in multiple batches.

4. Fry at 320°F for six minutes before turning the cookies over. Leave to cook an additional two minutes.

5. Remove the cookies from the fryer and allow to cool before serving.

# Chocolate-Covered Maple Bacon

**THE 2 SERVINGS CONTAIN: 359 CAL, 27.8 G FAT, 14.2 G PROTEIN, 1 G NET CARBS.**

## Ingredients

- ✓ 8 slices sugar-free bacon
- ✓ 1 tbsp. granular erythritol
- ✓ 1/3 cup low-carb sugar-free chocolate chips
- ✓ 1 tsp. coconut oil
- ✓ ½ tsp. maple extract

## Method

1. Place the bacon in the fryer's basket and add the erythritol on top. Cook for six minutes at 350°F and turn the bacon over. Leave to cook another six minutes or until the bacon is sufficiently crispy.

2. Take the bacon out of the fryer and leave it to cool.

3. Microwave the chocolate chips and coconut oil together for half a minute. Remove from the microwave and mix together before stirring in the maple extract.

4. Set the bacon flat on a piece of parchment paper and pour the mixture over. Allow to harden in the refrigerator for roughly five minutes before serving.

# Pumpkin Spice Pecans

**THE 4 SERVINGS CONTAIN: 177 CAL, 15 G FAT, 3 G PROTEIN, 1.5 G NET CARBS.**

## Ingredients

- ✓ 1 egg white
- ✓ ½ tsp. pumpkin pie spice
- ✓ ½ tsp. vanilla extract
- ✓ ¼ cup granular erythritol
- ✓ 1 cup whole pecans

## Method

1. In a bowl, stir together the egg while, pumpkin pie spice, vanilla extract, and granular erythritol. Toss with the pecans to coat, before transferring the pecans to the fryer.

2. Cook at 300°F for six minutes, occasionally giving the basket a good shake.

3. Allow the pecans to cool completely before serving. Keep them in an airtight container and consume within three days.

# Cinnamon Sugar Pork Rinds

**THE 2 SERVINGS CONTAIN: 253 CAL, 21.7 G FAT, 15.2 G PROTEIN, 1 G NET CARBS.**

## Ingredients

- ✓ 2 oz. pork rinds
- ✓ 2 tsp. unsalted butter, melted
- ✓ ¼ cup powdered erythritol
- ✓ ½ tsp. ground cinnamon

## Method

1. Coat the rinds with the melted butter.

2. In a separate bowl, combine the erythritol and cinnamon and pour over the pork rinds, ensuring the rinds are covered completely and evenly.

3. Transfer the pork rinds into the fryer and cook at 400°F for five minutes.

# Toasted Coconut Flakes

**THE 4 SERVINGS CONTAIN: 154CAL, 14.6 G FAT, 1.5 G PROTEIN, 0 G NET CARBS.**

## Ingredients

- ✓ 1 cup unsweetened coconut flakes
- ✓ 2 tsp. coconut oil, melted
- ✓ ¼ cup granular erythritol
- ✓ Salt

## Method

1. In a large bowl, combine the coconut flakes, oil, granular erythritol, and a pinch of salt, ensuring that the flakes are coated completely.

2. Place the coconut flakes in your fryer and cook at 300°F for three minutes, giving the basket a good shake a few times throughout the cooking time. Fry until golden and serve.

# Blackberry Crisp

**THE 4 SERVINGS CONTAIN: 485 CAL, 41.2 G FAT, 9.5 G PROTEIN, 1 G NET CARBS.**

## Ingredients

- ✓ 2 tbsp. lemon juice
- ✓ 1/3 cup powdered erythritol
- ✓ ¼ tsp. xantham gum
- ✓ 2 cup blackberries
- ✓ 1 cup crunchy granola

## Method

1. In a bowl, combine the lemon juice, erythritol, xantham gum, and blackberries. Transfer to a round baking dish about six inches in diameter and seal with aluminum foil.

2. Put the dish in the fryer and leave to cook for twelve minutes at 350°F.

3. Take care when removing the dish from the fryer. Give the blackberries another stir and top with the granola.

4. Return the dish to the fryer and cook for an additional three minutes, this time at 320°F. Serve once the granola has turned brown and enjoy.

# Churros

**THE 6 SERVINGS CONTAIN: 197 CAL, 17.4 G FAT, 4.1 G PROTEIN, 4 G NET CARBS.**

## Ingredients

- ✓ ½ cup water
- ✓ ¼ cup butter
- ✓ ½ cup almond flour
- ✓ 3 eggs
- ✓ ½ tsp. cinnamon sugar

## Method

1. In a saucepan, bring the water and butter to a boil. Once it is bubbling, add the almond flour and mix to create a doughy consistency.

2. Remove from the heat, allow to cool, and crack the eggs into the saucepan. Blend with a hand mixer until the dough turns fluffy.

3. Transfer the dough into a piping bag.

4. Pre-heat the fryer at 380°F.

5. Pipe the dough into the fryer in several three-inch-long segments. Cook for ten minutes before removing from the fryer and coating in the cinnamon sugar.

6. Serve with the low-carb chocolate sauce of your choice.

# Avocado Pudding

**THE 3 SERVINGS CONTAIN: 187 CAL, 18.2 G FAT, 2.1 G PROTEIN, 2.3 G NET CARBS.**

## Ingredients

- ✓ 1 avocado
- ✓ 3 tsp. liquid Stevia
- ✓ 1 tbsp. cocoa powder
- ✓ 4 tsp. unsweetened almond milk
- ✓ 1 tsp. vanilla extract

## Method

1. Pre-heat your fryer at 360°F.

2. Halve the avocado, twist to open, and scoop out the pit.

3. Spoon the flesh into a bowl and mash it with a fork. Throw in the Stevia, cocoa powder, almond milk, and vanilla extract, and combine everything with a hand mixer.

4. Transfer this mixture to the basket of your fryer and cook for three minutes.

# Chia Pudding

**THE 7 SERVINGS CONTAIN: 213 CAL, 17.5 G FAT, 4.5 G PROTEIN, 1 G NET CARBS.**

## Ingredients

- ✓ 1 cup chia seeds
- ✓ 1 cup unsweetened coconut milk
- ✓ 1 tsp. liquid Stevia
- ✓ 1 tbsp. coconut oil
- ✓ 1 tsp. butter

## Method

1. Pre-heat the fryer at 360°F.

2. In a bowl, gently combine the chia seeds with the milk and Stevia, before mixing the coconut oil and butter. Spoon seven equal-sized portions into seven ramekins and set these inside the fryer.

3. Cook for four minutes. Take care when removing the ramekins from the fryer and allow to cool for four minutes before serving.

---

# Bacon Cookies

**THE 6 SERVINGS CONTAIN: 117 CAL, 8.2 G FAT, 5.5 G PROTEIN, 2.5 G NET CARBS.**

## Ingredients

- ✓ ¼ tsp. ginger
- ✓ 1/5 tsp. baking soda
- ✓ 2/3 cup peanut butter
- ✓ 2 tbsp. Swerve
- ✓ 3 slices bacon, cooked and chopped

## Method

1. In a bowl, mix the ginger, baking soda, peanut butter, and Swerve together, making sure to combine everything well.

2. Stir in the chopped bacon.

3. With clean hands, shape the mixture into a cylinder and cut in six. Press down each slice into a cookie with your palm.

4. Pre-heat your fryer at 350°F.

5. When the fryer is warm, put the cookies inside and cook for seven minutes. Take care when taking them out of the fryer and allow to cool before serving.

# COOKING NOTES

Printed in Great Britain
by Amazon